Your Assumptions

How They Control Your Life &
What To Do About Them

Victor Bogart, Ph.D

Baskin Publishing Co., Eugene, Oregon

Library of Congress Number: 00-191464
ISBN #:   Hardcover   0-7388-2807-6
        Softcover   0-7388-2808-4

Author photo compliments of Richard May Photography.

To order additional copies of this book, contact:
Baskin Publishing Co. @ www.bogeybooks.com or
Xlibris Corporation
1-888-7-XLIBRIS
www.Xlibris.com
Orders@Xlibris.com

Contents

To Nikki
and all of you who insist on growing

Acknowledgments

I am indebted to my four highly effective collaborators—Deborah Loschiavo, Dennis Reynolds, Bruce Milletto, and the mystery woman behind the pseudonym Beth Cameron—for their participation. In every case, I was delightfully surprised by their willingness to share on the record so much of their professional and personal lives. Without their enthusiastic and complete cooperation, this would be a different book. Their contributions add so much of value that I hesitate to think what this book would be like without them. I feel honored to bring each of them into these pages and your awareness.

To my editor, Anne Fox, I am indebted for a good deal more than her meticulous and painstaking editing. Before Anne, I thought I was a pretty good writer, so I expected that the original manuscript I sent to her would come back with minor corrections but generally unchanged. As I often do, I had set myself up with my faulty assumptions for a rude awakening. The manuscript came back loaded with the red ink of many corrections and suggestions. While most were minor, a surprising (to me) number were major ones that led to my cutting away some 20-30 percent of excess fat, a consequence of my tendency toward loquaciousness where silence or a simple sentence would suffice. Thanks to Anne and the rewriting that her editing encouraged me to undertake, I was able to find my proper voice for this book. And, in the course of our working together, I gained an excellent teacher and a friend.

To Charlie McGee of Signal Design I am indebted both for his graphic artistry and his patience in putting up with my every whim. While I claim credit for *the idea* of putting the faces of willing friends and relatives on the cover—along with many faces selected from the Art Explosion library CD-ROM—it was Charlie's creative skills that gave it life.

To Lisa Adams of Xlibris, my gratitude for facilitating a smooth collaboration between our two publishing firms. And to Xlibris for making available its digital publishing and Internet services.

To my men's group, my thanks for their emotional support.

And last, but also first, to my wife and companion, Nikki, my deep appreciation for putting up with all the consequences of my indulging a writing career.

About the Author

Victor Bogart is one stubborn crit-
ter. Not only has he managed to survive into his eightieth year in excellent health and spirits, he persists in
writing books that bring fresh ideas,
new ways of looking at everyday human behavior, and self-helpful suggestions for how we can improve our
lives. *Your Assumptions* is such a book.
It is also one of two published works*
and two more in process that trace
their origins to the early 1960s and their rich content to Vic's
professional life as psychotherapist and teacher.

Vic earned his Ph.D. in Counseling and Gerontology at
Oregon State University, 1985—at age 64!, and holds master's
degrees in Social Work (University of Washington, 1966) and
Journalism (University of California at Berkeley, 1962). His
years as journalist, psychotherapist, teacher, and author of
nonfiction self-help books add up to half a century and counting.
But it is the melding of ALL the varied experiences of his life,
together with his optimism, humor, and wisdom that he freely
shares with us in his writing.

You can learn more about Vic Bogart and his works by (a)
reading this book and (b) logging on to his Web site: *http://
www.bogeybooks.com*. You can also contact him via his e-mail
address: *vicbogart@aol.com*.

Vic and his wife Nikki live in Eugene, Oregon.

* Vic's first book, *Odyssey: A Psychotherapist's Journey Along the Cutting Edge,* was published in 1993. For more information, go to the Web site or e-mail address above.

Introduction

*To me, an assumption is when you have all your ducks in a
row and you're sure you know enough to conclude that it's safe
to assume something. Frankly, I think the word "assumption"
is a time bomb, and it will go off! Believe it!*

—Nikki Bogart

The purpose of this book is to make you aware of a common habit
you tend not to notice until *bam!* a bucketful of cold water hits
you in the face. At that moment you have to deal with the effects
of a faulty assumption.

For the most part, we don't realize how our assumptions direct
the way we will respond to any situation in any given moment.
We are also largely unaware of how we come by our assumptions,
how they shape what we think and do, and what we can do about
them.

This book is designed to help you know more about the awe-
some potential of your assumptions—for both good and ill—and
thereby to gain more control over your daily life and your destiny.
Toward these ends, this book is structured much like a three-act
play:

·   The first act (Chapters 1 and 2) instructs you about the
    nature of assumptions and offers an operational definition of
    what they are, how we come by them, and how they work.

·   The second act (Chapters 3 through 7) raises the curtain on
    a variety of major adult-life scenarios wherein our assump-
    tions shape our thoughts, our attitudes, and our behaviors.

These chapters examine in depth the impact of our assumptions on our Self-definitions or self-concept, Personal growth, Marriage, Aging, and Death and Dying.

- The third act (Chapters 8 through 12) brings you a series of conversations with four men and women who are success stories in their respective professions. In interviews with the author, they share their fascinating experiences and the assumptions that enable them to function as effective leaders in their chosen fields of Childcare, Special Education, and Executive Management in the two worlds of the large corporation and small business.

- An encore (Chapter 13) offers you a small taste of a new way of thinking about your assumptions and how they work together to shape the various aspects and dimensions of your personality.

- And to make the book's content more personally relevant to you, each chapter closes with a *What To Do About Them* section that invites you to explore how you can apply this knowledge in your own life.

This book will not save you from making faulty assumptions. No book can do that, nor do I believe it would be a good idea even if it were possible. As I see it, our most effective learning tool is our ability to recognize when we're making assumptions that turn out to be incorrect and counterproductive. That recognition has broad potential, from allowing us to correct a minor error in judgment on the one hand, to making major changes in our lives on the other.

When the time bomb of a flawed assumption goes off, as my wife Nikki promises it will, it may have the potential to close out your life or hurl you into a whole new world of fresh realizations and experiences. Our faulty assumptions can devastate our lives in ways we neither anticipate nor wish for. But they can also teach us with their hard lessons of correctable experience and enable us to grow beyond them to become who we wish to be.

I hope you find this book to be a powerful assist in your quest.

—Vic Bogart

1

About Assumptions

Topic Index

1
About Assumptions

Assume *v.t.* **-sumed, -suming. 1.** to take for granted or without proof; suppose; postulate; posit.
Assumption *n.* **1.** something taken for granted; a supposition. **2.** the act of taking for granted or supposing.
Assumptive *adj.* **1.** taken for granted. **2.** characterized by assumption.

—Random House Webster's College Dictionary

Assume *v.t.* **1.** To make an **Ass** of **u** and **me**.

—expression in common usage

The Titanic is unsinkable is a dramatic example of an assumption's power to drive a giant ocean liner into an iceberg and send its occupants to lifeboats and safety or to death. Examples of such major assumptions that don't hold up fill the pages of history, but the ones that most frequently make an **Ass** of **u** and **me** are the smaller, personal ones we come up with ourselves.

What do you mean, "Where was I?" (I assumed) We were to meet at noon under the clock in front of Macy's!

I ended our relationship because (I assumed) you didn't like me or approve of the way I live my life.

I'm so sorry! I assumed my job interview was for 10 o'clock tomorrow, not 10 o'clock yesterday.

Do these examples sound familiar? Each of us has written on the pages of our own histories countless examples of having paid the price for mistakenly taking something for granted. More often than not, we give little or no thought to most of our assumptions. They are largely invisible to us and out of our awareness until something happens to draw them to our attention.

With this book you can become aware of the assumptions that are driving your life, understand where they come from and how they work, and learn how to do something positive about them. In short, the purpose of this book is to help you steer clear of the icebergs.

Why Your Assumptions Matter

Without exception, all of our assumptions are products of our imagination, expressions of our mind's ability to take things for granted, to suppose, without proof, that things are so.

Our assumptions are our best efforts to make sense out of the events in our lives. We may *experience* them as *reality*, but in fact they are all "in our minds." We only *imagine* them to be provable realities, to be true or false. Because we are so good at bringing our imagination to life, we often endow our assumptions with the same lifelike quality that we experience in our favorite movies and theatrical performances. When we watch a really good magician, we can't believe that what we see is only a well-contrived illusion.

Even more important, your assumptions—and everybody else's—are the source of all conscious and much unconscious behaviors. From our assumptions flow our acts of kindness and love, but they are also at the root of all our misunderstandings, prejudices, fears, hatreds and acts of violence.

I'm afraid of you because [I assume] *you intend to do me harm.*

I'm uncomfortable around people who are [black, white, brown, homosexual, of the opposite sex] because [I assume] *they are different from me.*

I squooshed that spider because [I assumed] *it would bite me.*

Behind each of our acts we can find the assumptions we are making about the particular situation to which we are responding. Change our assumptions and our view of the situation, and the way we respond also changes. Our assumptions shape our perceptions and behavioral responses. This fact answers the question: *Why are our assumptions important?*

Whoops a Daisy!

More often than not, we take most of our assumptions for granted. Once we accept their validity, we do not question them until something overturns our expectations.

There was a time when I really believed [I assumed] *you would always be faithful.*

When I was young, I thought [I assumed] *I would live forever.*

I thought [I assumed] *the day would never come when . . .*

Think about your own life. Think of when you assumed you knew what was going on, only to discover that you were operating on a mistaken assumption. How many times have you incorrectly assumed that someone in your life would never do this or that? Dozens? More than that? And how much pain have your misjudgments created for you?

The price we pay for our faulty assumptions can be great indeed. Marriages derailed. Loves lost or never pursued. Friendships broken or never begun. Personal dreams and great potentials left behind. Fortunes lost or never made.

And that's only at the micro level of our individual lives. On the macro level we live in a world where too many of our assumptions feed racial, religious and political animosity and intolerance with consequences that endanger civilization and life on earth.

While you may feel impotent to do much about assumptions being made and acted upon at the macro level, at the level of your personal life you *can* accept responsibility for your own assumptive processes. You *can* reduce the price you are paying in pain and unhappiness for your outworn and faulty assumptions.

Assumptions Bring Consequences

Assumptions, by their very nature, are hypotheses. They are never more or less than our best guesses about everything from A to Z. Assumptions can be major or minor, of worldly import or not, of deep and lasting consequence, or of limited and momentary significance. But regardless of size or significance, they all carry consequences. Of course, the little ones have minor consequences, such as,

I thought (assumed) *this street would be a shortcut to the railway station.*

As a rule, the bigger the assumption, the bigger the consequences.

The world was flat (an assumption) *until it was proven to be round.*

We know that for a long time men feared to explore beyond their known world because of an accepted assumption that it wasn't a globe but more like a pancake. In a similar way, our assumptions place boundaries and limitations upon how we think, feel, and behave. All assumptions are valid and operative only within prescribed limits.

Assumptions Impose Limits

The power of assumptions to limit our exploring beyond their boundaries keeps us safe from imagined and feared unknowns. Every one of our personal histories is littered with *Don'ts!* that we dutifully or fearfully obeyed. More often than not, behind every *Don't!* loomed a frightening assumption foretelling harm or regret if we chose to *Do* instead. No doubt many *Don'ts* served us well. Still, there may be prohibitions we obeyed that leave us thinking we should have played those cards differently:

I should have married my college sweetheart.
I should not have married when I did.
I should have . . .

Each of us faces the challenge of making our own best choices from among the countless *Do's* and *Don'ts* suggested by our assumptions. Either way, the choice always limits our understanding and experience of what is possible. But as Columbus and many others demonstrated when they challenged the *world-is-flat* assumption, whole new worlds exist beyond the horizons of our assumptions. To bring our new worlds into view, we need only the courage to question and explore the boundaries of our self-limiting notions.

Upended Assumptions: The Banana Peels of Humor

Bud Abbott: *Strange as it may seem, in baseball they give ballplayers very peculiar names. Nicknames. On the St. Louis team we have Who on first base, What on second, I Don't Know is on third . . .*
Lou Costello: *That's what I want to find out. I want you to tell me the names of the fellas on the St. Louis team.*
Abbott: *I'm telling you: Who's on first, What's on second, I Don't Know is on third.*
Costello: *You know the fella's name?*

sA

Abbott: *Yes*
Costello: *Then who's the fella playing first base?*
Abbott: *Who.*

In Abbott and Costello's time-honored and hilarious *Who's on first?* comedy routine, Costello is relying on the assumption that Who and What, etc., have their normal meanings. Abbott's responses are based on the assumption that these are the players' nicknames.

Humor counts on the clashing of contrasting assumptions. The process is always the same: we are set up (or sucked in or lured) along the garden path of one premise and then flipped over on the banana peel of a contrasting premise. What makes it comedy instead of tragedy is that we are expected to laugh. Abbott and Costello are comedians, and we naturally *assume* that they are out there doing their shtick for our entertainment. If Costello falls flat on his face on stage, we are prepared to find it funny. If he should fall flat on his face from a heart attack, that would be tragedy; nevertheless, if we assume his fall is just part of the act, we laugh.

We all know of instances where we responded inappropriately because we were operating from a wrong assumption.

All Our Assumptions Play Tricks on Us Sooner or Later

As mentioned earlier, all our assumptions lose at least some of their accuracy and relevance over time because we generate them at particular moments in our personal histories. They provide us with the most acceptable explanations of events happening in our lives at that moment.

My earliest recollection is of my daddy telling me the tooth fairy left the dime under my pillow in exchange for my missing tooth. I believed him. [I assumed he was telling the truth.]

At the time we accept our assumptions, they are as close as we have been able to come to an understanding of "what's real." They become our "reality."

And this brings us to a tricky part. Once we have accepted an assumption-based belief as "reality," we resist uncovering and reassessing the underlying assumptions, even to accommodate new information. If we do not understand the connections between assumptions and reality and how they operate, we tend not to think about underlying assumptions. We stumble along from one "reality" to the next, sticking with the one at hand until the banana-peel effect turns our world upside down.

When I was nine, my belief in the tooth fairy, along with my belief in Santa Claus, came to an abrupt and painful end. My four sisters and three brothers and all the children in the neighborhood taunted me for being such a baby.

Of course, a nine-year-old's belief in Santa Claus and the tooth fairy is a relatively minor disconnection. The disconnections have greater consequences as we age.

For example, I write this at a time when the stereotypical belief of my older generation of men is that "real men" are always strong, tough, powerful and masterful. Gentleness, compassion, tenderness, expressions of affection toward other men, etc., are "weak, feminine" traits to be avoided at the risk to one's "manhood." I absorbed this concept of "male as always powerful" as a teenager from the culture around me, from my role models and from my peers. Because I assumed they all knew what they were talking about, I accepted this model of adult masculinity as the reality I had to measure up to. And for many years I made myself miserable, knowing that I couldn't measure up because I often failed the "always powerful" test.

Time has passed, and this narrow definition of adult masculinity is no longer in vogue. But so long as I and my brothers hold on to our outworn assumptions and beliefs about the nature of maleness, we will continue to experience the pain and guilt of our assumed inadequacies.

Selling Assumptions Is Big Business

Many elements in our free-market economy profit from our willingness to buy into someone else's assumptions. Advertising executives, politicians, big chunks of the legal profession, stockbrokers, car salesmen, profit by persuading us to buy their assumptions—and *their* products—rather than someone else's. The advertising industry in particular reaps its millions by designing and redesigning appealing assumptions to induce us to choose this or that pair of jeans, bottle of perfume, pair of running shoes, or automobile.

> *Wear Nike shoes and leap tall buildings!*
> *Drive a BMW, and your dream woman (or man) will float down from the sky and into your life!*
> *Smoke Marlboros, and become a Clint Eastwood!*

More often than not, only after we take the product home and live with it for a while do we discover that, as with watching a magician saw a woman in half, we bought into an illusion.

In 1936 Elmer Wheeler, an advertising pioneer, set down *Principle Number One of Salesmanship*:

> *Don't sell the steak; sell the sizzle. It is the sizzle that sells the steak and not the cow, although the cow is, of course, mighty important.*

Perhaps we can, with some justification, blame Elmer for the fact that we consumers have been subjected to one helluva lot of sizzle ever since. For our day-to-day well-being, we must keep our senses sufficiently honed so we can differentiate the sound of the sizzle from the quality of the steak.

Revising Assumptions—A Never-ending Process

Because all assumptions are, at best, approximations of "reality," there is always some degree of error built into them. Reducing the degree of error in our assumptions is one of life's never-ending challenges.

The longer our assumptions go unchallenged, the more likely they will accrue greater error rather than less. We generate them (accept them, take them on) at particular moments in our lives, and they are based on our best judgments about the meaning of events at that moment. As time passes—as we and our understanding of events shift—the old assumptions are likely to lose their original relevance.

It was easier for our parents than it is for us to fix in place the "facts of life." The rate at which things change was slower for them and even slower for their parents than it is for us in today's world. The consequence of our parents' world changing less rapidly offered tangible support for their assumptions for longer periods than it does for us. In today's Information Age, frequent review and revision of all assumptions are appropriate to reduce their degree of error and to limit the probability of catastrophic occurrences.

Boeing Says Vapor Threat
Requires a Tank Redesign

BALTIMORE, DEC. 9—In an effort to prevent explosions like the one that caused the crash of Trans World Airlines Flight 800, Boeing officials said today that the design of the company's jetliners needed to be changed to guard against the buildup of flammable fumes.

. . . Daniel Cheney, a Federal Aviation Administration expert in propulsion systems, said that "ever since aviation began," *designers have simply assumed* that the fuel tanks held a flammable mixture and have instead designed planes to prevent sources of ignition. "That *assumption of flammability* has been successful but not successful enough," he said. Now, he

said, the government and airlines will look for ways to reduce
the flammability of vapor in the tanks. (Italics added)
                                                        —*The New York Times,*
                                              Wednesday, December 10, 1997, p. 1

Today, assumptions are being updated and revised much more
extensively and rapidly than we can keep up with. Car manufac-
turers regularly recall thousands of cars to fix things we assumed
were going to work. The tobacco industry constantly recalculates
how it's going to sell its lethal products to an increasingly better-
informed public. And so on.

Because life involves constant change, and because our everyday lives are rooted in assumptions based on information gathered
by our senses, our assumptions are always in danger of lagging
behind the latest information.

Oh, if only I'd known that, I'd have done something different.
He didn't hear the news report that the bridge was out, so he drove
the car into the creek.

We check on the latest weather reports and the state of our vehicle's
traction devices to decide if it's safe to drive over a mountain pass in
winter. We should also check on the trustworthiness of the rest of our
assumptions, an easy task in this Information Age.

Consider your assumptions to be a garden from which sprout all
your ideas, many of which will flower into the accomplishments of
your life. As long as your garden of assumptions is not weeded, thinned,
and fertilized with new information and understanding, you will har-
vest the bitter fruit of your outworn assumptions. When our lives are
not going as well as we would like—when we are in pain because of a
troubled relationship, unhappy in our job situation, depressed over
how we are feeling about ourselves—it's time to pay attention to the
assumptions we are buying into. Just as our automobile won't run
forever on old parts and little maintenance, it's a sure bet that our
old assumptions need inspection and a tune-up, if not replace-
ment.

WHAT TO DO ABOUT THEM

Suggestion: Use the blank Notes & Comments pages that follow for your answers to this chapter's *What To Do About Them* questions. Doing so will allow you to review your responses as you progress through this book to see how well they hold up for you. Perhaps they will stand the test of time. Perhaps you'll find they won't.

A basic message of this chapter (and of this book) is: *Your assumptions are the shaping source behind everything you think and do.* The following questions can help you consider how true this basic message may be for you:

1. Think of one or two current situations in your life that are not going as well as you would like. Ask yourself, *What assumptions am I making about this situation?* For example:

    Situation:
    My relationship with my supervisor at work.
    Assumptions of mine:
    1. She (he) doesn't approve of my work.
    2. I think she (he) would be happy if I quit.
    3. She (he) and I don't agree on how the job should be done.

2. Ask yourself, *Can I think of situations in my life where assumptions of mine do not come into play?*

Notes & Comments

Notes & Comments

2

The Assumptive Process

Topic Index

2
The Assumptive Process

In this chapter we focus on the assumptive process: How our assumptions shape our perceptions of the events affecting our daily lives and our thinking, feeling and behavioral responses to such events. But first, let's clarify the distinction between our assumptions, on the one hand, and our perceptions, emotions, and various cognitions (including our values, beliefs, observations, opinions, and judgments) on the other.

Operational Definition of an Assumption

How can you tell the difference between an assumption and a thought, belief, value, perception, or feeling? What, if any, is the difference between "knowing" something is true, "believing" it to be true, "feeling" it to be true, or "assuming" it to be true?

To clarify the difference, the following is the definition of an *assumption* as the term is used in this book:

An assumption is one or more thoughts, feelings, perceptions, beliefs, conclusions, or other form of information that becomes the initiating premise for a response to an event.

To state it in a different way, an assumption is an *activating set* of thoughts, beliefs, etc., that takes active form as an assumption when it generates a behavioral response.

For example: I may harbor beliefs and feelings about snakes that lead me to be fearful of them. But it's only when these beliefs and feelings about snakes cause me to leap out of the way of one, or to strike out at one with a weapon, that my thoughts and emotions about snakes take active form—become operational—as an assumption.

Figure 1 illustrates the distinction. The seven circles of mental activity depicted in the diagram generate the information from which we draw the assumptions that move us to act. The seven circles of mental activity interact both with each other and with the assumptions they generate.

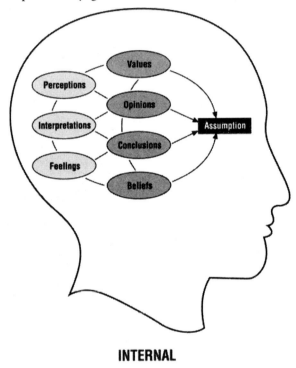

INTERNAL

Figure 1

Your Assumptions Initiate Your Behaviors

All of the activities by which we generate our stores of information and form our assumptions, as represented in Figure 1—

perceptions, feelings, beliefs, etc.—are happening internally. But it is our assumptions that trigger us to do what we do.

Figure 2 represents both the *internal* processes from which we generate our assumptions, diagramed in Figure 1, and the *external* processes set in motion by our assumption-triggered behavioral response to events taking place in our lives.

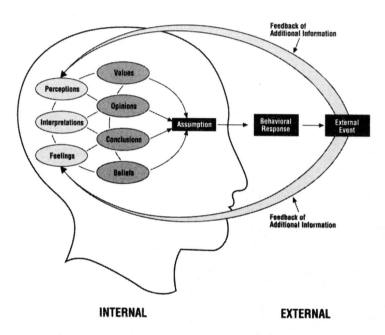

Figure 2

For the most part, we are largely unaware of the processes depicted in Figures 1 and 2. We usually don't pay attention to how come we do what we do. As the expression goes, *Shit happens!* to which we respond in ways that make the most sense to us. But in every case it is our assumptions that are the cause of our behaviors.

Figure 2 shows how our internally generated assumptions lead us to specific behaviors (the *Behavioral Response* box) that in turn result in an event happening *externally* (the *External Event* box). This external event, in turn, generates additional information for us (the two huge arrows labeled, *Feedback of Additional Information*). It's important to note that the way we perceive and respond emotionally to this additional information may or may not influence our preexisting assumptions.

We can respond in different ways to the new information coming from the impact of our behavior on our external environment. A lot depends on how open we are. Or to put it another way, our responses will be limited by how tightly we hold onto our preexisting assumptions.

Admittedly, it's often easier to hold onto an old assumption than to let go and allow it to be modified. Benefits can be had from remaining fixed in place by one's unchanging assumptions: We can feel secure and safe "knowing" that our understanding of things is as it should be, and we needn't be bothered with having to question and accept the risks of change. Although we may be indulging in self-delusion, so long as it works, it can seem preferable to our imagined painful alternatives.

Making the Connection Has a Big Payoff

By understanding that our assumptions trigger our conscious behaviors, we can look behind a specific behavior and ask the question: *What is (are) the assumption(s) triggering this behavior?* Theoretically, we can ask this question of each of our behaviors. And, of course, it can be asked of everyone else's behaviors as well. But only if and when the question is asked can we find the answer and understand the true meaning of the behavior.

Properly linking specific behaviors to the assumptions that brought them forth offers at least two big rewards. The first:

When we correctly understand the meaning of a specific behavior, we can avoid all the tangles that come about from misunderstanding.

For example: If your best friend informs you that she saw your husband dining with another woman and your husband denies it, whom do you believe?

Is your husband hiding something? Is your friend mistaken? Is she really your friend or trying to stir up a fuss? Until you can clearly understand what actually happened and how come, such a tangle can be an emotional bear trap that can cripple and hold you fast. And clear understanding calls for understanding everybody's assumptions that explain everybody's behaviors.

The second big reward:

By properly linking behaviors to their underlying assumptions, we can respond to problems at the level of what's causing them.

When we respond only at the level of a problem's surface appearance, *i.e.*, its symptoms, the problem is likely to recur rather than be resolved. For example: In the hypothetical situation of your best friend and your husband, if the facts and underlying assumptions are not examined and clearly understood, your relationships with both friend and spouse are likely to be damaged, perhaps ruined.

Your Assumptions Have Power and Inertia

In response to the feedback of additional information from our external environment, our assumptions rise up to exert their influence on our perceptions, thoughts and emotions. This reaction is a resisting force to modifying one's assumptions.

Inertia, as defined by the discoverer of the laws of gravity, Sir Isaac Newton, is the tendency of bodies at rest to remain at rest and of bodies in motion to remain in motion until acted upon by an external force. Our assumptions, although they are not physical bodies, nevertheless often seem to possess inertia: they tend to remain fixed in our minds until we modify or nullify them in response to further inputs of information. Our assumptions tend to remain in place by exercising their power to shape subsequent feelings, perceptions, thoughts, etc.

If your mother believes (assumes) that you are ruining your life by living according to your lifestyle rather than hers, she will probably continue to "see" you doing that until she *allows* new information and understanding to modify her beliefs (assumptions).

An assumption seems to perpetuate itself by accruing self-justifying evidence, as much as to say, *See, I told you so!* The assumption's internal feedback loop reinforces its power and leads the assumer to conclude that the assumption is totally reliable and need not be reevaluated.

Your Assumptions Shape Your Cognitive Processes

Cognition, n. 1. Act or process of knowing; perception. 2. The
    product of such a process; thing thus known, perceived, etc.
                    —*The American College Dictionary*

All of our cognitions—our thoughts and perceptions—are channeled and shaped by our underlying assumptions.

When the 17th-century mathematician and philosopher René Descartes said, *I think, therefore I am,* he acknowledged that thinking is at the root of our human identity. In this book, we will venture a step further by extending Descartes' statement with one of our own: *I assume and thereby define who I am being.*

The ability to think allows us to identify ourselves as human. *What* we are thinking shapes our human experience. And what we are thinking is shaped and directed by the particular assumptions we accept from all of the possibilities presented to us by our experiences.

Our assumptions are our best guesses about everything of any size, import or consequence. Because they shape how we perceive, think, feel and behave, the assumptions we accept and act upon define how we will view our world, how we will think about it, and what we will choose to do in it.

> *The four-minute mile was an assumptive barrier to runners for many years until Roger Bannister transformed the assumption to: "It can be done and I want to be the one to do it!" And with training, dedicated effort and help from pacesetters, he broke the imaginary barrier.*

In the years since, many another miler who now "knows" (assumes) that the four-minute barrier no longer exists has joined Bannister in running faster. But we all have barriers in our lives. Too many of us accept the assumption that we cannot stretch beyond the confines of who we think ourselves to be and what we think we are capable of doing. We all have our personal four-minute mile we can yet run, no matter what our age or circumstances.

Your Emotional Power Plant at Work

> *Your teenage daughter left a note saying she would be home by 10 or call if she was detained. Now it is well past midnight, and you still haven't heard a word. Your anxiety has been mounting as minutes pass. Fear, which you have been pushing to one side, now surges in like a tide, sweeping over your reason with imaginings that blind you like a dark, impenetrable fog. As the minutes drag on, your hopes tangle in a desperate struggle with your fears to control events whose reality remains in doubt.*

Or, again:

> *You overhear a conversation not meant for your ears that immediately shatters your world as you know it. You find yourself struggling for breath, your blood suddenly pounding in your head. Time hangs motionless. You don't know whether to stop your ears or sharpen your hearing to not miss an awful word, whether to move*

a muscle or slide under the table. A jumble of emotions—shock, disbelief, humiliation, fear, rage—sweeps you away to a reality far removed from where you were a short time before.

Events such as these remind us that our unexpectedly violent emotional responses can leave us feeling victimized and helpless. The language we use to identify our more powerful emotions shows how easily we can regard ourselves as being at their mercy: *head-over-heels in love . . . driven mad . . . lifted to heights of exultation . . . swept away by passion . . . overwhelmed by grief . . . moved by tenderness . . . transfixed by fear . . . plunged into despair . . . tormented by guilt . . .*

It's as if our powerful emotions are the result of outside forces we are helpless to do much about. And again, we use familiar words to refer to our helplessness: *compelled . . . addicted . . . victimized . . . overwhelmed . . .*

Such language suggests that we are innocents upon whom our more intense emotions inflict their own will. We tell ourselves (and others) that our passions have a life of their own and that we are their victims. We say things like *I got carried away,* or *It wasn't really my fault,* or *The devil made me do it.* We can disclaim responsibility for our emotions and justify our behaviors, but we risk prolonging our victimization and perpetuating our helplessness. By acknowledging ownership of our emotions and behaviors, we can do something about the most troubling ones. To not do so, is to live with a time bomb.

When you understand the processes that give rise to your emotional responses, you can accept ownership of them and be more forthright in considering their implications for your life. Emotional honesty empowers you. It establishes and maintains healthy levels of self-esteem. And such understanding begins with taking responsibility for examining the underlying assumptions that trigger your emotional responses. Your powerful feelings, whether they be anger, disappointment, rage, fear or grief, are all linked to your perceptions, your way of thinking about your situation and the assumptions that color and shade all of them.

Hot-button Issues

We all have "hot buttons." When they are pushed, we tumble out of emotional control. The usual source of such powerful emotional response is some prior deep wounding or violation to our sense of self. Abandonment, betrayal, violation of one's physical or emotional integrity, can open wounds that remain raw and sensitive to the touch for years. Sounds, smells, faces, situations, can act as painful, unexpected reminders that our wounds are not completely healed.

Nowhere are these hot buttons more evident than in persons suffering from posttraumatic stress. Whether the trauma is a consequence of war, rape, death, divorce, or other violent events, we are always left with the hot buttons. And while some of us may feel we escaped serious injury in our lives, none of us is entirely free. We are all walking wounded, and we have the buttons to prove it.

Our hot buttons remind us that we still have personal work to do. We can use them to ask ourselves if, perhaps, now the time has come to get on with the work.

A good way to get on with it is to look more closely at our emotions in the context of our assumptive processes.

Acknowledging and Exploring Your Emotions

Acknowledging your emotional responses allows you to explore their meanings and accept them as expressions of where you are in your life now. That's easier to say than do. Suppressed feelings come in packages of many shapes and colors, and some of them set off alarms in our emotional early-warning systems. To open those packages of feelings is to risk exposing ourselves to shame or guilt or helplessness or worse. And what is to be gained by opening them up? Who says we're going to survive the resulting explosion? And if we do survive, who says it's going to be any better on the other side?

Good questions.

But irrelevant.

We are all caught in Life's little game of *Truth or Consequences*, and the questions, good or not, assume we can avoid facing the truth without paying the consequences.

Usually, we just go along not opening the potentially explosive package. Or even better, we deny that it has even arrived. And that may seem to work for a while. But Life has its ways of showing us that the consequences of *not* opening the package are also real, painful and not likely to vanish as we want them to. Most of us end up avoiding the truth until the consequences force us into a very tight corner where acknowledging and opening the package becomes less painful than any other alternative.

We all have examples of how this has worked in our own lives.

I was a two-pack-a-day smoker of cigarettes for 35 years. Smoking felt good, and those feelings were an essential part of the identity I was working hard to create. So were the feelings that came with two-martini lunches and a host of other activities I generated with the hope of illuminating and adding panache to my existence. I was always trying to generate feelings that were reassuring and comforting. And for a very long time I refused to acknowledge that I was resorting to self-destructive behaviors in my attempts to enlarge those feelings of self-worth.

Finally, in my mid-forties, after 30 years of inhaling 438,000 cigarettes, more or less, my midlife crises forced me to open and examine some of my time bombs. Only then did I understand how I was using this particular addiction to con myself into believing that my cigarette-smoking scenarios were vital to my identity.

It took another several years—and a doctor's warning that my lungs had become "pre-emphysemic"—to let go of the smoking habit for good. But at least I faced those latter years with more self-awareness and honesty.

Connecting Emotions to Assumptions

Our emotions are the expressive outpourings of the assumptions our intellects make.

I am a classical-music nut. Whenever I can, I have classical music playing in the background throughout the day and night. I write by it, prepare my meals by it, eat by it, sleep by it.

My emotional responses to classical music are as varied as the music itself. I have absolutely no intention of changing my emotional responses to this dear companion. But if I did, I would have to explore the assumptions I have been making that enable my emotional responses to pour forth. Memories that come to mind range from childhood to adulthood:

> . . . my earliest years with a warm and caring foster family, where older children practiced classical piano and violin
> . . . later years when my mother took me to Saturday morning children's concerts put on by the Chicago Symphony Orchestra
> . . . still later years as a member of a young-adult music-appreciation group in Montreal
> . . . still later, the World War II years of attending concerts in London's Royal Albert Hall.

And always, classical records playing symphonies and sonatas on my radio. Classical music fills my life.

My assumption underlying my emotional responses?

> Classical music creates for me a safe, nurturing, familiar world filled with passion, excitement, peacefulness, serenity, and creative muses singing their unutterably sweet melodic musings.

If I wanted to change the nature of my emotional responses to classical music, I would have to do something about my assumption. But to want to do that, my current emotional responses would have to become extremely distasteful. Like my current responses to cigarette smoke.

WHAT TO DO ABOUT THEM

Suggestion: Continue to use the blank Notes & Comments pages that follow to write down your Q's and A's, as well as thoughts you wish to record for later perusal.

1. Do you understand the operational definition of an *assumption?* (You may wish to review the material on page 33)
2. Do you understand how the *assumptive process* works? (You may wish to refer to pages 34-36)
3. Do you understand what a *hot-button issue* is? (Refer to page 41) Can you identify one or more of your hot-button issues and their underlying assumptions? For example:

Hot-button issue:
I get extremely angry and explode at my partner when he (she) messes up the house and doesn't clean up the mess.

Underlying assumptions:
1. My partner never thinks about my needs.
2. He/she is being extremely selfish.
3. I'm being taken advantage of and used.
4. It is his/her responsibility to clean the house and keep me from having these terrible feelings.

Suggested Assignment:

Practice delaying your behavioral response when your *hot buttons* get pushed. Defer reacting to your assumptions and allow additional information to flow in.

Your immediate goal is to break a hard-wired pattern. You can learn to do this by consciously trying to interrupt your impulse to react spontaneously and allow yourself the luxury of calming down so you can consider your situation in a different light. You might try the proverbial "counting to ten," or you might walk into the garden or imagine yourself in a favorite place in nature or start dancing . . . Allow yourself to experience what happens if you experiment with "keeping an open mind" instead of "leaping to a conclusion."

Note: In preparation for your next hot-button reaction, write down four alternative actions you can choose to take:

1.
2.
3.
4.

Notes & Comments

Notes & Comments

3

Self-defining Assumptions

Topic Index

3
Self-defining Assumptions

From waking in the morning to putting the cat out at night, we make hundreds of decisions and each decision is based on one or more assumptions. Most of our assumptions are so automatic that we don't pay attention to them until something goes awry. This ongoing assumption-making activity of ours is vital and necessary to our functioning as thinking human beings. Without it, we would be stopped dead in our tracks. Imagine having to pause and make a conscious decision about every step we are about to take as we proceed through our day. The activity we now pack into five minutes would take an hour. Without our ability to trust that our world will continue as we assume it will, we would be immobilized.

The Assumptions We Make About Ourselves

Among the many assumptions we make each day, one class of assumptions has an overwhelming impact on the lives of every one of us: the assumptions we make about ourselves. These are the assumptions by which we define:

- *Who we think we are*
- *What we think we are capable of*
- *What we think we deserve*
- *What we think we can expect from our lives*

Our self-defining assumptions are at the core of many of our beliefs about ourselves and our attitudes and behaviors toward all the other people and events in our lives.

Among these core assumptions are often self-limiting ones that get in our way. These are the assumptions that lead us to see ourselves as *less than* and that are a constant source of much of our discomfort, pain, and sense of failure. These are the assumptions that lead us to say things like:

"Oh, I couldn't possibly do that!"
"I'm not smart enough to . . ."
"I'm too old to . . ."

The poems, plays and novels waiting for us to give them life will never see the light of day, so long as we *assume* ourselves to be incapable of generating them. The potential creative artist, teacher, doctor, lawyer, accountant, administrator, engineer, scientist buried within never materializes because we *assume* ourselves incapable of fulfilling such dreams.

Just look around you at the people in your world. How many dreams and possibilities are going unfulfilled because the dreamers have fallen victim to self-limiting assumptions that block their paths? And what possible scenarios are lying dormant in your own life because of your self-limiting assumptions?

Core Assumptions

The phrase *core assumptions* calls for clarification. Just think of an apple. What you see is the outside skin, blemishes and all. At the core are the apple seeds that have the potential to generate other apple trees. But the seeds are not visible to the naked eye unless the apple is opened up. Core assumptions are analogous to apple seeds in that they have the power to generate other assumptions that are similar to themselves and are usually out of sight until the apple is opened and examined.

We define core assumptions as: *Deeply rooted, strongly held beliefs that give rise to a host of other assumptions consistent with the core assumption.*

Some examples of core assumptions:

· *A belief in the Bible as the literal word of God*
· *A belief that white people are more intelligent than people of color*
· *A belief that females are the weaker sex*

Each of the above assumptions gives rise to multiple assumptions that are consistent with it. For example: A core assumption that the Bible represents the literal word of God gives rise to hosts of other assumptions through which translations of biblical text become the sole arbiter of human belief and behavior. The core assumption that white people are more intelligent than people of color spawns a colony of other assumptions leading to multiple scenarios in which white human beings dominate nonwhite human beings. The core assumption that females are the weaker sex germinates hosts of similar assumptions by which a male-dominated society is sustained.

Self-defining core assumptions work in a similar fashion. Some examples:

· *I truly believe I am capable of accomplishing whatever I set out to accomplish.*
· *I have a strong belief that I am not very bright.*

A core belief in your ability to achieve your long-term goals fosters other optimistic assumptions that allow you to set and achieve shorter-term goals and purposes. Similarly, a core assumption that you are hampered by a wanting intelligence will foster related assumptions that are likely to undermine and sabotage your attempts to achieve your dreams.

Finding Hidden Assumptions

Many self-defining core assumptions may be out of our awareness because we acquired them during our formative years and have long since become used to them. Although they may be buried in our unconscious, they are still alive and powerful, directing how we regard ourselves. And while we may think they will remain hidden from us short of months or years on a psychiatrist's couch, they are readily discoverable. They really can't hide if we want to find them. The trick is to know where to look. And good places to look for them are *behind* surface behaviors.

For example: One place to look for core assumptions is behind our more intense emotional responses.

> *Ellen, age 43, chose a career as a professional librarian largely because she preferred the quiet and serenity of the library to the loud and jarring world outside. For Ellen, shouting and confrontation triggered emotional upset and sudden urges to shrink and withdraw. When depression set in, she sought help, and it didn't take long for her to uncover some core assumptions of which she had been unaware, including a belief that it was "wrong" for her to manifest her power in a direct way. Her fear of shouting and confrontation was both a fear of violating her core assumption that it was "wrong" and a fear of her own unexpressed power.*

Keep this in mind the next time you find yourself responding to a situation with unexpected intensity: If you find yourself emotionally aflame, you can be sure (assume) the flame is being fed by an inner stockpile of fuel. It may be one of your hidden core assumptions catching fire.

Another place to look for hidden self-defining assumptions is behind those unequivocal statements of belief we find ourselves passionately defending as *true* or *natural* or *given*. This is not to argue with the merits of your beliefs but to suggest that if you look behind your responses, you are likely to discover assumptions of which you were unaware.

> *Steve, age 44, takes pride in being a successful lawyer. His wife Monica is currently suing him for divorce, culminating a stormy seven-year marriage. This is Steve's third unsuccessful try at marriage, and the experiences have left him bitter, angry and depressed.*
>
> *Living as a single adult in a small apartment, alone for the first time in years, Steve recently joined a men's support group sponsored by his church. During the three months since he joined the group, Steve has come to see himself differently in some key respects.*
>
> *In the past, he almost always saw himself as being in fierce competition to succeed in a world that was anything but friendly. He found support and reinforcement for his core assumption that "life is a battle" from his male friends and the activities and interests they all shared.*
>
> *Now, in the support group, he has been opening up his emotional life to men he respects who don't share this core belief. As a result, he is coming to see more clearly how his deeply ingrained competitive drive not only steered him into the legal profession but reached into every other corner of his life as well. He is coming to see in a somewhat different way how his "lawyer's mind" has both sharpened his adversarial and confrontational skills and has turned him into a fierce opponent in his marriages rather than a collaborative partner.*

Core assumptions, such as Steve's deep-rooted belief that his survival and success require him to be a skilled adversary, do not easily disappear. Until they are modified or replaced, they continue to breed their little apples, their offspring, their look-alikes in different clothing. For example: During their marriage, Steve and Monica were trapped in a scenario of endless argument over relatively minor issues, such as whether or not they should buy a new car or new furniture, or who is leaving dirty dishes in the sink, or why they are unable to manage on their income. Sometimes the arguments were settled, sometimes just avoided, but always new disputes arose to replace or be added to the old. Because Steve's core assumption was never surfaced and dealt with, his "natural" commitment to competing and winning the battles with Monica persisted, and the pattern of the marital relationship between them didn't change.

Self-limiting Thinking

Recently, I was enjoying a pleasant evening at the home of a friend who was playing host to a visiting couple from out of town. The four of us had finished dinner perhaps an hour before, and I was beginning to lapse into my usual postprandial poop-out. I got to thinking:

It's nine o'clock.
I'm probably keeping these folks from retiring.
They're too polite to ask me to leave.
Tomorrow is a workday. I should get to bed so I can get up early.

This line of thinking became so convincing that within a short time it led me to bid goodnight to what was a very nice visit with people I care about.

I acted from thoughts that seemed reasonable and appropriate. But even as I was walking to my car, I recognized that parts of me did not want to leave and were quite unhappy. When the realization struck that tomorrow was Sunday and I didn't have to get up to go to work after all, my inner voices *really* put up a fuss. Some hours later, those unhappy voices were keeping me awake and angrily accusing me of stupidity, bad manners and lousy judgment.

More to the point, I had acted on the basis of assumptions

without having done anything to check them out. After all, how did I know that *I'm probably keeping these folks from retiring?*

I could have asked, *At what time are you planning to retire?* The question, awkward as it may be, could have led to a more open discussion and agreement on when our get-together should close down for the night. Such discussion probably would have put an end to my rising feelings of discomfort.

Not checking out the underlying assumption led to emotions and behaviors that had unhappy consequences for me and perhaps for the others.

And what about those other assumptions that lay behind or beneath the obvious one? For example: *What led me to the assumption that I was standing in the way of their being able to retire?*

I recall that the thought was prompted by a lull in the conversation and the stirring of some feelings in me of discomfort. But why did I assume that my presence was somehow an inconvenience?

I don't have to dig too deeply to get in touch with those familiar negative self-judgments I generate whenever I'm uncomfortable in social situations. Thoughts like:

I'm not measuring up . . . (to whatever I think I'm supposed to measure up)

I don't really belong . . . (to whatever or whomever I'd really like to belong)

The Negative Power of Negative Thinking

Negative self-judgments such as these come too readily for too many of us. That readiness is maintained through repeated use over a long period that usually stretches back into the recesses of our trauma-pocked childhood. And I rarely meet anyone whose childhood wasn't laced with trauma.

The power of such negative self-judgments manifests in their consequences. Their major consequences are that they impose severe limits on our ability to consider a wider range of more positive options. And they make us miserable.

In the previous example, the self-judgments that *I'm not measuring up* and *I don't really belong* were confirmed by my withdrawing from the scene. I was not measuring up to my own expectations, and I ceased behaving as if I really belonged. All of my energy was focused on proving the correctness of my negative self-judgments. Gone were the other possibilities for enjoying the evening in the company of people I care about. We might have danced all night, we might have laughed and sung, we might have created the beginnings of a happy future together. As it was, my negative thinking and unchecked assumptions led me to shut down my ability to see and consider other options. All I could focus on was my discomfort and my not wanting to intrude my continued presence in a situation where I was *assuming* my presence might no longer be desired.

Layering Assumptions

In the example of having cut short my visit with my friends, we can see at least two distinct layers of assumptions and their corresponding layers of derivative thought. At the most evident level, the one closest to the surface, is my thought that *I'm probably keeping these folks from retiring,* which also expresses my assumption that they wished I would go home so they could go to bed.

At this level, assumptions and their derivative thoughts are quite visible. If we are of a mind, we can easily recognize them and do something about them right away or, upon reflection, a little later.

At a deeper level, the picture is more complex. There are connections between the thought, *I'm probably keeping these folks from retiring,* and the deeper-level thoughts, *I'm not measuring up* and *I don't really belong.* The first was my interpretation of a current event in progress. The latter two sound more like habitual statements of belief I was making about my worth as a person. They sound like the kind of negative self-judgments I have been struggling with for most of my life. In all likelihood, there's a self-limiting core assumption to be found at a deeper level that surfaces as a self-esteem issue I have yet to deal with.

The assumptions we make about ourselves are at the core of our self-esteem problems, at the heart of our successes and failures in every activity. It follows that our self-defining assumptions are key to unlocking the doors to all our hopes and dreams. For this reason, we will continue to examine our self-defining assumptions in the chapters that follow, each of which focuses on a different aspect of adult life.

WHAT TO DO ABOUT THEM

Suggestion: Continue to use the Notes & Comments pages in responding to the assignments and questions that follow. Remember, there's no one right way to respond to these exercises; there's only *your* way.

The following exercises can help you identify some of your beliefs about yourself, the core assumptions from which your beliefs spring, and some basic steps you can take to examine and assess their current validity for you.

1. Complete the following sentences with as many statements starting with the word "I" as come to you. [Examples are shown in brackets]

   a. *My life would be much better if only . . .*

   [. . . I were rich.]

   [. . . I hadn't married my current partner]

   b. *I can't make the changes in my life that I would like to make because . . .*

   [. . . I am too old]

   [. . . I don't have a college education]

2. Examine each of your responses to 1a and 1b to see how many of them you can use to complete the sentence below. These statements of belief about yourself are some of your core assumptions.

   a. *I assume that I . . .*

   [. . . would be (different, happier, etc.) if I were rich]

   [. . . would be (happier, etc) if I hadn't married my partner]

   [. . . am too old to change]

   [. . . am blocked for lack of a college education]

3. Explore the history and validity of each of your assumptions about yourself in 2a by responding to each of the questions below.
   a. *How did I come by it? (When? Where? From whom?)*
   b. *What leads me to think the statement is still a valid one?*
   c. *What leads me to think the statement is no longer valid?*
   d. *What steps can I take to check it out?*
   e. *How has it shown up in my life?*
   f. *What effect has it had on my life?*

Notes & Comments

Notes & Comments

4

Assumptions About
Personal Growth

Topic Index

4
Assumptions About Personal Growth

We are all learning creatures, and the opportunity to learn is always present. However, the extent to which we are able to use our learning opportunities depends largely on the assumptions we make about ourselves as learners and about our options.

> *Sarah assumes, for whatever reasons, that it's useless for her to apply for that open position or for that available scholarship, and the learning opportunities that could follow her application remain closed to her. Sonya, for whatever reasons, makes opposite assumptions about herself and takes advantage of her opportunities.*

When it comes to the assumptions we make about ourselves as learners, Sarah and Sonya represent two classes of folks: *Those who make positive assumptions* (Class 1) and *Those who make negative assumptions* (Class 2). In addition to the first two classes, there is also a third class of personal-growth assumers that I would think most of us fall into: *Those who make **both** positive and negative assumptions.*

Depending on which of the three classes you happen to fall into, the task you face varies.

For those of you in the first class of strictly positive assumers: Well done! Stay tuned to your assumptions about yourself as a learner and Go For It.

If you are in the third class of people who variously make positive and negative assumptions about your ability to learn and grow, your task is one of tuning in to how you are responding to your situation of the moment, identifying your assumptions as positive or negative, and then dealing with them as your situation warrants. If your assumptions are positive, go with them; if they're negative, examine why and make the necessary shifts.

For those of you in the second class of strictly negative assumers: Pay attention, good buddy. You have an opportunity to turn your world around right here.

So, Class 1: You may be dismissed, and we'll see you in Chapter 5. Of course, you may stick around, if you wish, and maybe learn something.

Class 2 and Class 3: We have work to do, but I assure you that it can be done and most probably will be very rewarding for you.

Opening Your Eyes to Opportunities

Our eyes are closed to opportunities that we fail to recognize as opportunities. In fact, opportunities to feed and nourish our normal hunger to learn and grow are happening for us every day, in every hour, in every moment. How do you know that this very moment in your life *doesn't* offer you an opportunity to learn something new and different about yourself? Or an opportunity to explore a path you've never walked before? You *won't* know unless you open your eyes and your mind and your heart.

> *For the first time in years, Harry is feeling anxious and severely threatened. Acme Nuts & Bolts, the company for which he has worked for the past 23 years, is being acquired by a larger corporation and is about to be downsized. Harry is fearful that he is on the list of employees soon to be sacked. At age 53 and still years away from retirement, he is not prepared to be thrown out onto the street and forced to compete for a new job in today's highly competitive marketplace. Until now, he felt secure in his job and never seri-*

ously considered looking for a better one. He performed well enough in his current situation to be rewarded with periodic, if modest, position and pay increases—and well enough was good enough for him. Betty and the kids were always the most important part of his life, and the job provided a good home and a decent standard of living. And his hobby of woodworking and furniture making fleshed out what he regarded as a near-perfect life. Now, his world seems to be turning upside-down. For the first time in many years, he is terrified by what the future may hold.

Clearly, Harry is responding to the possibility of losing his job. He has negative assumptions about his future prospects. His situation and his negative assumptions are understandable, and he is by no means alone in the world with them. But he is quite unprepared to face the risks and dangers that probably await him, and he finds himself staring into his crystal ball. He imagines dark and threatening demons staring back. Because his mind and eyes are closed to the positive possibilities of his situation, Harry is unable to see them.

Harry fits in as a member of Class 2, the negative assumers. At least so far as he relates to his job situation, he holds only negative assumptions about himself as a learner and grower.

If, like Harry, you are closing your mind and eyes to your learning opportunities, the likelihood is that you are fearfully holding on to where you are in your personal learning curve. You are probably feeling that it's better to hold on to whatever you've got than face the horrible consequences of risking and failing (or however you describe the anticipated negative outcomes of your negative assumptions about yourself). Both you and Harry have your eyes shut tight and are strongly denying that growth opportunities exist for you. But your denials may not be all that strong! A little letting go of your negative mindsets and perceptions and convictions might be enough to do it. As those of you in Class 2 learn to trust in your essential goodness and the positive potential within you, the darkness you now see in your crystal ball will lighten with renewed hope, positive thoughts and unforeseen opportunities.

If, on the other hand, you're in Class 3, swinging back and forth between optimism and pessimism, you at least know what it feels like to see yourself in positive terms and to make positive assumptions about yourself as a learner. When you're in your negative mode, you don't see opportunities to learn and grow; you see stumbling blocks and hazards. But as you switch from negative to positive assumptions and perceptions, the learning opportunities emerge.

What Will Your Personal Growth Look Like?

Six months have passed in the lives of Harry, Betty, and their three children, and Harry was indeed laid off. For a while, things were as bad as Harry had envisioned. Getting fired was just as traumatic as he thought it would be. He felt as if he had been thrown onto the scrap heap of the rejected and unwanted, and his self-esteem drained away as if the bottom had dropped out of the vessel that contained it. What Harry hadn't foreseen was how important his job had been in providing a steady stream of that vital psychic fluid called self-esteem. Weeks went by during which he did little but brood and mourn, and nothing Betty could say or do helped much. His woodworking hobby gave him an occasional lift, but more often than not he lacked the incentive and energy for it.

Fortunately, Harry had come away from Acme Nuts & Bolts with enough of a separation package to permit him some grief time. But the weeks of grieving were followed by frustrating months of reading classified ads and fruitlessly chasing job interviews. Harry was spiralling down more deeply into depression and helplessness. Then one evening at the dinner table, Betty came up with a suggestion that got him thinking in an entirely different direction.

"How about starting up our own business around your woodworking?" she said. "You could work at what you know you like to do, and I could handle the office-type stuff. The kids are going to be

out of the nest before long, and I'm going to have to find something to fill the Mommy gap."

Betty's suggestion made sense to Harry, and before long the two of them were visualizing how such a family enterprise might work. Without realizing how the change had come about, Harry was feeling hopeful and energized. Who could know how it would all end?

Generating a vision of your mission is a beginning place. But as Harry and Betty are in the process of learning, there's more to going into business together—or achieving any other mission in life—than coming up with a vision. The vision is prerequisite, but making plans, setting goals, discovering how and where to acquire needed knowledge and skills, and learning to apply them are also among the necessary steps Betty and Harry will have to take. By then, this pair of budding entrepreneurs will be seriously involved in their own learning processes and well along the self-developmental path they have chosen.

And how about you? What will *your* pathway to further personal growth look like? What dreams or goals do *you* have tucked away? Do you have a vision of who you want to become five years from now? Are there neglected parts of you that you'd like to explore and develop? Do you have a secret desire to attend law classes at night and become a lawyer? A tap dancer? A sculptor? A trombone player? A rock star? A chef? If so, can you visualize changes you would like to see happen to bring that about?

If you pay attention to your dreams and visualize the steps along the path, you can begin the process of growing that new and better future for yourself.

Three Influencing Factors

Unique experiences in your life contribute to how you regard your own personal growth, but three factors influence the assumptions of every one of us: our age, our role models, and our culture.

1. The age factor

[**Note:** You can find a more complete treatment of assumptions about aging in Chapter 6.]

> *Until the bottom dropped out of his life at Acme Nuts & Bolts, Harry, at age 53, hadn't thought of himself as no longer in his prime. But finding himself suddenly out on his ear and among the unemployed gave rise to disturbing assumptions about aging. After yet another frustrating day of job hunting, he would make comments to Betty like:*
> *"They only want young people."*
> *"As far they're concerned, I'm over the hill."*
> *"I must be too old for this rat race."*

We all tend to assume that the older we get, the fewer options we have. But that's because we don't see the many fresh opportunities that open up as we age; we only see all those options disappearing that go along with being younger, more desirable, perhaps more physically fit, and less burdened by the baggage of time. Of course, some options attach more to being younger, such as giving birth and climbing Mt. Everest, but even these are constantly being challenged by people who flaunt those old assumptions and establish new limits. We tend to continue to measure ourselves against old standards rather than look for the new ones we can set as we get older.

At any age, personal growth results from exploring the previously unexplored, opening up territory in our lives that we haven't previously paid much attention to. Harry and Betty are exploring the creation of a husband-and-wife business partnership. What territory might you explore?

2. The role-model factor

The role models in our lives exert powerful influences on our assumptions about our personal development. Role models provide the patterns and templates that we hold up and emulate or reject as we learn how to negotiate the paths of our lives. They inspire us to stretch, to reach. Parents, grandparents, teachers, mentors who favored us with their positive encouragement, guidance and caring have probably influenced us beyond our realization. The absence of such positive models have contributed to the difficulty we may be having in dispelling our negative assumptions about ourselves and our potentials for further growth and development.

Becoming aware of the role models whose patterns you have chosen to emulate or reject, is a step toward freeing yourself to generate your own creative variations. Remaining unaware of your role models blinds you to why you behave and respond as you do and blocks you from giving up the old patterns that limit or cripple your ability to explore new avenues. Such blindness can also prevent you from appreciating the many gifts that your role models have bestowed upon you. If the gift of love and loving was among them, you are blessed. If the gift of honoring your unique strengths and potentials was also among them, you are doubly blessed. And if the gifts of optimism, joyfulness, and responsibility were also among them, you are indeed endowed with treasures enough to create your own golden pathway.

3. The cultural factor

My 1965 copy of Random House's *American College Dictionary* defines *culture* as "*the sum total of ways of living built up by a group of human beings, which is transmitted from one generation to another.*"

But this definition is too sweeping and generalized for our purposes here. If we are to examine how the cultural influences in our own lives help shape our assumptions about personal growth, we need to recognize that we live in a world consisting of many cultures, large and small, and each of us is influenced by more than one. We each belong to one or more "dominant" cultures—African, Asian, American, European, Protestant, Catholic, Jewish, etc.—and to one or more subcultures—tribe, gang, family, group, neighborhood, school, workplace, house of worship, institutional setting, etc..

> *Harry's 23 years at Acme Nuts & Bolts taught him a great deal about surviving and succeeding at Acme. One of the things Harry learned was that, as one of the firm's 350 employees, he could find his own comfort level and settle in without being singled out or drawing too much attention to himself. It was as if he could remain anonymous, as if he wore camouflage that allowed him to blend into the background.*
>
> *Probably the major reason for Harry's comfort at Acme was that it "felt familiar" to him. It felt a lot like his service in the Army after he graduated from high school: he easily learned and obeyed all the rules, he got along well with his buddies, and he felt at home in the Army. Although he wouldn't have used such language to describe his Army experience, Harry fit in with its customs, folkways, mores, conventions and lifestyle.*
>
> *And Acme also felt as familiar to Harry as his childhood homelife had, where his dad worked in a factory very much like Acme while his mother maintained a safe and nurturing home for her husband and for Harry and his younger sister, Adele.*

Until Acme kicked him out of the nest, Harry had managed to maintain his familiar cultural environment throughout his adult life. It was not an environment that rattled his cage, so to speak; it didn't jolt him out of his comfort zone to where he might generate a vision of himself as a different or better person than he already was.

We are all like Harry in that the way we think about our own growth is shaped by, among other factors, our cultural experiences. In their various ways our cultures let us know how we should regard ourselves, which of our behaviors are acceptable and which are unacceptable, and which of life's infinite pathways should open to us and which should be closed. Our cultures set forth their rules for the game of life they prefer that we play. Whether we play by their rules or whether we march off to the beat of different drummers is up to us.

Preconditions of Personal Growth

The principal precondition for personal development is dissatisfaction with the way things are. If you are a happy camper in one of life's Rest Areas—as Harry was at Acme—personal development is not likely to be a high enough priority to motivate you to get out of the Rest Area and back onto the highway.

Remaining in the Rest Area long after its advantages have worn off can be much like holding onto an addiction. If you're addicted, you have to hit bottom before you can recognize and let go of the illusion that the addictive option is the only one open to you. It's like continuing to watch used-car commercials on TV without a mute button: no matter how much discomfort the commercials inflict, you are not moved to switch channels until it becomes unbearable.

Extreme discomfort—pain—may be the best motivator for moving you to undertake the really important changes. We tend to assume that pain is an unfortunate and negative element in our lives. This fundamental assumption leads us to avoid pain at all costs, even when its consequences for us are distinctly positive. Far better to assume that pain is a vital and necessary warning signal that something is wrong and needs to be fixed.

Three other preconditions for personal growth, in addition to discomfort and pain, are: *1. The degree of importance; 2. Your level of motivation; and 3. Your clarity of vision and purpose.*

1. Priority

Unless your personal growth is a matter of concern to you, unless it holds a place of importance in your awareness, you won't be consciously involved in its development. Without conscious involvement, you forfeit control of your progress along your growth path, and you abdicate responsibility for charting your own future. The higher up on your priority list, the more attention your personal growth needs will clamor for, and the more attention you are likely to give them.

2. Motivation

Although we all have the ability to learn, your motivation to learn is what drives you to exercise your ability to grow. Without motivation, little or no movement is likely.

As we said above, pain may well be the primary motivator in moving you to undertake basic changes in your life, but other motivators are also available to you: *enthusiasm, curiosity, spirit of adventure, the excitement of experimentation, hunger for differentness and newness.* Any or all of these can instill in you the sense of urgency to propel you beyond your current limits.

3. Vision and purpose

If you accept the assumption that every person is born with a mission, then you have to ask of yourself: *What is mine?*

Once you can identify and visualize a unique mission for yourself, it can serve as an organizing principle for how to go about using your energies and resources. When Harry and Betty began to identify and visualize going into business together, they were beginning the process of reorganizing their lives to bring about the fulfillment of their particular mission.

Harry and Betty's new mission called for a major break with their past that would involve many changes in the way they managed their daily lives. But the lack of a major mission in your life need not stall you. More limited goals and visions provide good practice for the time when a larger sense of mission presents itself to you. And these smaller efforts may turn out to be the seedlings from which larger ones can grow .

Grappling with Your Blocks to Personal Growth

Why haven't all those quick fixes you've tried in the past worked in a lasting way?

Because many of your blocks to personal growth are ideas about yourself that are deeply rooted in your mind, and the quick fixes usually do little more than scratch the surface. It's like trying to get rid of the moles in your lawn by plugging up their holes. You may feel you've accomplished something and have overcome the problem, but the moles are as happy as ever in their cozy little hidey-holes and can hardly wait to provide you with more holes to fill.

But you can do better.

Your blocks—the deeply rooted ideas about yourself that frustrate your attempts to improve your life—can be brought to the surface, examined and re-evaluated. Instead of feeling blind-sided by your repeated inability to make lasting progress, you can take control over your blocks and, one by one, modify or replace them. Where you think there is no way, there are ways that you simply haven't found as yet.

Remember that all of your blocks—your deeply rooted ideas—are assumptions that are highly vulnerable and subject to change. They are not immutable even though you feel they are. They can be changed and replaced in the flicker of a fresh insight, a flash of a fresh vision, a surge of new knowledge that floods into your awareness with the dawn of a new day.

WHAT TO DO ABOUT THEM

1. Chapter 4 identifies three classes of people who make assumptions about themselves as learners: Those who make positive assumptions (Class 1); those who make negative assumptions (Class 2); and those who make both positive and negative assumptions (Class 3).
   a. Identify in which of the three classes you see yourself.
   b. What assumptions are you making about yourself as a learner?

2. Given your assumptions about yourself as a learner:
   How do you see the future course of your personal development at this time?

3. This chapter makes the point that our assumptions about aging can influence the beliefs and attitudes we make about ourselves.
   a. What are some of your assumptions about aging?
   b. How do your assumptions about aging enter into your beliefs about yourself as a learner and into your personal development plans?

4. This chapter observes that our role models play a big part in shaping our assumptions about ourselves as learners.
   a. Identify as many of your role models, both positive and negative, as you can.
   b. Think about what you have learned from each of them about yourself as a learner.
   c. How pleased are you with the lessons or gifts you have received from each of them?
   d. What are your current feelings toward each of them?

5. Cultural influences play a large part in shaping our assumptions about ourselves as learners and about the personal development paths that are open to us.

a. What would you regard as your dominant culture(s)?

b. What subcultures can you identify as playing a role in your life?

c. What influences in your dominant and subcultures can you identify as having significantly shaped your assumptions (i) about yourself as a learner? (ii) About the social and occupational roles open to you?

6. Each of us has the capacity to generate a sense of our mission.

   a. What can you say about your own sense of your mission?

   b. How clearly are you visualizing your mission?

   c. On a scale of 1 to 10, how strong is your motivation to achieve it?

   d. What plans are you making to fulfill your mission, and how would you rate your progress at this point in your life?

Notes & Comments

Notes & Comments

5

Assumptions About Marriage

Topic Index

5

Assumptions About Marriage

The fate of every marriage—indeed, every relationship between two people—is rooted in their respective assumptions about themselves, each other and their relationship. Where assumptions are unclear, unstated and conflicting, the relationship stumbles and struggles with disappointments and misunderstandings, and breakdown of the relationship is likely. Where assumptions are clear, mutually understood and compatible, the relationship is rewarding, and its lasting success is likely.

In no other arena of your adult life are you as likely to step on the land mines of clashing assumptions so frequently as in your marriage. Without conscious effort to check out your own assumptions and those of your partner, you are destined to wander unwittingly into minefields where your own ignorance is likely to have explosive consequences. The land mines come in all sizes—little ones that can ruin your day and big ones that can mortally wound your marriage—and they are capable of exploding at any moment. And all have the potential to break hearts, shatter faith, cause recrimination, foster guilt, and cripple relationships.

What's Love Got to Do With It?

Everything!

In most cases, love's presence or absence is THE major determinant of the course and fate of marriages. Our basic need to love and be loved drives us into marriage on the promise of it, into misery and despair or the arms of other lovers when marriage fails to deliver it, into bitterness and divorce when marriage has failed.

And what is love if not total surrender to what feels absolutely right and natural? In terms of our assumptions, love can be defined as a surrendering to the proposition that the two of us will live out our dreams of a perfect match.

The *acts* of loving demand commitment, giving, caring, supporting; but the *emotion* of love is a releasing of oneself to one's passion. We accept that the emotions we are feeling (and the assumptions from which our feelings spring) are so overwhelmingly right that we willingly relinquish control.

Love, with a capital L, is all powerful. But our brightly burning passion has a life of its own and will burn for only as long as the fuel that feeds it. Time inevitably tames the wild passions, and then we have to rely on what we can create and build in the everyday to sustain our marriage.

Our assumptions about our marriage are put to the test in the daily goings on, the proving grounds of marriage.

About this Chapter

In this chapter we meet three couples: Darlene and Dana, a young couple marrying for the first time; Lois and Eric, a couple in midyears marrying again after divorce; and Vince and Nora, an older couple marrying in late adulthood.

We examine the assumptions each couple brings to the marriage, we note how they arrived at their assumptions, and we predict how their assumptions are likely to affect their marriages.

Young Marriages

We bring to our first marriages in young adulthood the hopes, ideals and dreams of our growing-up years. We also bring the particular assumptions about marriage that we have come away with from the marriages of our parents and other role models.

If you fit into this age group, you may share with each other much or little about the particular assumptions that led each of you to the decision to become husband and wife. The realities of your marriage as they unfold provide you with the evidence against which you will test those assumptions and measure the successes and failures of your relationship.

Reality always impacts upon the assumptions you carry into your marriage. Because first marriages rely on dreams and imagination, the impact of actual events on your dream-based assumptions can lead to a rude awakening. Your response to these rude shocks depends upon the awareness and resilience you and your partner can muster to communicate about and adjust your assumptions.

Unfortunately, the odds are against you. Statistics show that a shocking percentage of marriages fail. According to the U.S. National Center for Health Statistics, for every two marriages celebrated in 1994, for example, one divorce was granted. And in the years since, it appears that the marriage-failure rate has been going up. Statistically, you have less than an even chance that your marriage will not end in divorce.

The high failure rate strongly suggests that assumptive resiliency among our current crop of marriages—the ability of marital partners to make needed revisions of their marital assumptions to accommodate the realities of their marital experience—is inadequate to the task it needs to accomplish. If you hope to be on the winning side of the statistical battle, paying attention to your assumptions is a good way to go.

Darlene and Dana

Darlene was 19 and Dana was 21 when they married. They had met two years earlier at a senior prom at Centerville High, where Darlene was a sophomore and Dana, a senior. Each had come to the prom with a different date, but when Dana asked Darlene to dance, a spark was struck that later ignited and flared. Their romance waxed and waned over the next two years while Darlene remained in high school and Dana attended Centerville Community College. On the second anniversary of their meeting and just prior to Darlene's graduation from high school, the couple again attended the senior prom, at which Dana proposed to Darlene.

Darlene said, "Yes." For her, the spark of love had flared and burned nonstop. She saw something of her father in Dana: strong, attractive in a lanky way, and relaxed and confident in social situations. It was important to Darlene that her parents liked and approved of him as a husband for her. She felt that they had managed a successful marriage, and now she hoped to do the same with Dana. Over the past two years she had come to regard him as mature and responsible, a man she could easily love and devote her life to making happy.

Dana was ambivalent. He had been battling reservations about tying himself down too early in life. He still carried scars of a stormy home life that culminated in his parents' divorce when he was 13, and he didn't want more of that. His dad had walked away from the marriage and had withdrawn to the margins of Dana's life, leaving Dana with a legacy of anger and bitterness. But he felt sure that he loved Darlene, that he had strong reasons for getting married: she was beautiful, their sex was great, she was devoted to him, and he was sure she would be the perfect wife and mother for their children. Nevertheless, he felt strongly that life was meant to be an adventure to enjoy and not a heavy burden.

If the two of them had thought in terms of examining their basic assumptions about their marriage, they might have stated them as follows:

Darlene:
· *Marriage with Dana will answer my dreams and fulfill my life.*
· *Dana and I share a total commitment to make our marriage a*

good and fruitful one that will last forever.
· *I want to be a mother like my mom.*
· *I can fully trust Dana to fulfill his vows and can depend on him to take care of me and our family, as my dad did.*
· *I will make him happy and successful through my loving him and by being fully supportive, considerate and agreeable.*

Dana:

· *Marriage is a risky proposition and can get in the way of living a fulfilling life.*
· *Darlene and I love each other, we are both special and good people, and we should be able to make a good marriage.*
· *My desire for a relaxed, leisurely and carefree life is a bit of a problem, but all single young men feel that way, and it's about time I grow up and take on the responsibility of a family.*
· *Darlene makes it really easy for me to have what I want, and I'm sure I can continue to count on her for that.*
· *I shouldn't have a problem controlling the urges I get for other women.*

Assessment and predictions

Because Darlene reveals no ambiguity about marrying Dana, her assumptions are likely to hold her to her marital commitment so long as she continues to regard Dana as her Prince Charming and the actual events taking place in their marriage don't shatter her illusions and her faith in it.

On the other hand, Dana's assumptions reveal a potential conflict between his marriage and what he regards as a fulfilling life for himself. If the marriage with Darlene gets to look more like his parents' marriage than one that promises the fulfilling life he idealizes, he will probably succumb to his urges and pull away.

Influencing young marriages in particular are the roles and degree of involvement of parents and in-laws and the couple's responses to them. Struggles can be frequent and stressful over how dependent or independent of their parents and in-laws young marrieds will choose to be. Darlene's positive assumptions about her parents and their marriage may or may not suggest an overdependency on them and an unwillingness to break away on her own. Dana's experiences of growing up in a troubled marriage and abandonment by his father may or may not be a source of trouble for them. At this point we don't have a clue about the role in Dana and Darlene's marriage his parents will play, nor how well the two of them will balance the needs of their marriage and the demands of their parents.

Another major influence on young marriages is their response to parenthood. Darlene's assumptions suggest she will be a strong and positive mom. On the other hand, Dana's growing-up experience with his own father provided him with a negative role model; he may have a lot to learn about healthy parenting. And his desire for a relaxed and carefree life may get in the way of that.

Unless Dana and Darlene allow their assumptions to be modified through awareness and communication about them, the two of them will have to deal with their problems while holding on to their original assumptions. In that case, chances are that Dana will defect from the marriage and Darlene will have to look elsewhere for her dream husband.

Marriage at Midlife

Second or subsequent marriages at midlife have the advantage that you come into them as a veteran.

If your first marriage left you a widow or widower, then you may have acquired a built-in model of a successful marriage that ended in the death of your partner and left you carrying the scars of a tragic loss.

If your first marriage ended in divorce, you carry the model and memories of a conflicted marriage in which your marital differences could be resolved only by abandoning them.

In each case your original assumptions about marriage have been tested and reforged by your experiences.

The challenges of marriage at midlife center around our developmental struggles familiarly referred to as our midlife crises. You can expect major shifts in values, goals, occupational directions—in short, reversals and rearrangements of the basic assumptions of you and/or your spouse. If most of your midlife turnabouts have been accomplished prior to marrying, you have already let go of much of the dead wood of your respective pasts and are now sharing fresh and more current values and goals. Such marriages tend to fare better than the ones in which you are trying, once again, to fulfill the failed dreams of your youth. If your earlier marriage failed because your assumptions were faulty and you're still clinging to them in their unmodified state, your later marriages are not likely to prove them right.

In addition, stepparenting and parenting issues are likely to be a more powerful influence in the early stages of midlife marriages than in first ones. Among the reasons:

· Competing parenting styles can generate difficult problems for the marriage and the new family unit. These problems can be difficult to resolve because the parenting habits (and assumptions) of both partners are already well established and entrenched by their previous parenting experiences.

· Where a new stepdad comes into an established family, the children's needs can assume greater concern for the mom than for the stepdad, and complications can result. Depending on their ages, the children's parenting needs and conflicting emotions around acquiring a new parent are—and ought to be—of primary concern for both parents.

Lois and Eric

Lois and Eric are coming into their second (for her) and third (for him) marriages with the benefits of experience and maturity that midlife brings.

Lois:

Age 35, married at 17 to Barry, a childhood sweetheart, divorced two years ago after 16 years of marriage.

Three children: Ann, 18 (Lois was pregnant with Ann at the time of their marriage); Barry Jr., 15; Cecilie, 13.

Ann just graduated from high school and is about to go off to college.

Barry Jr. decided a year ago that he wanted to live with his dad, and both parents support his freedom to make this choice. Barry Sr. has not remarried but has been going with Rebecca, also divorced for some time, and the two of them are living together, so that Rebecca is available to Barry Jr. as a stepmom. So far, it's an arrangement that seems to be working well.

Cecilie ("Cecie") lives with her mom but spends alternate weekends and optional vacation time with her dad.

Lois has a longing for drama in her life. She looks back on her marriage to Barry as having started out as exciting, but the excitement soon drowned beneath the routine and drudgery of raising the children. The precipitating events leading to divorce were extramarital affairs on both their parts.

Divorce released Lois into a springtime flowering of renewal and exploration. During the next two years she joined an athletic club and began working out regularly in the exercise room and pool. She joined her community's Actors Playhouse and appeared as a supporting player in a local production of the musical Oklahoma. *And she signed up for a scuba-diving course and met Eric, the man she was to marry a year later.*

In retrospect, Lois sees her marriage as having failed from boredom and a growing conviction that Barry didn't live up to her need for an exciting life partner. Now her dramatic longings have been rekindled in her new romance, and she looks forward to her marriage to Eric with a fresh confidence. She feels that communication between them is of a quality that she and Barry never achieved and that the two of them share a commitment to explore fresh and exciting territory together.

Eric:

For as long as he can remember, Eric has loved the thrill of adventuring where most men wouldn't dare. As a youth, he was a mischievous hell-raiser. By now, at age 45, he has climbed Mt. Kilimanjaro, scuba-dived beneath the Arctic ice pack, and single-handledly sailed a small sailboat from Hawaii to San Diego. Eric is a likeable man who has always managed to find jobs to support his adventuring: hired hand at yacht clubs, crew member on expeditions, instructor of sailing, skiing or scuba-diving. On two occasions he made and sold documentary films of his adventures.

Eric has also been married twice (to Estelle and Maggie), but both marriages failed to survive the onslaught of his seven-year itches and his urges to venture forth. With each of his partners he managed very good three-year stretches, but trouble brewed in the latter years when his wanderlust and involvements with other women shredded the love and trust that had previously supported both Estelle and Maggie. Because he had chosen to have a vasectomy, there were no children from either marriage.

For the past several years, Eric has been experiencing a midlife transformation. He feels his life slowing to a less hurried, more considered pace. He experiences himself as more mature and responsible than before. And while his thirst for adventure is still strong, he now sees himself adventuring with a life partner rather than alone. Since connecting with Lois in his scuba-diving class a year ago, he has been longing to settle down and become a father to Lois's children. And he and Lois have been talking about the possibility of having his vasectomy reversed.

Assumptions

If Lois and Eric had thought in terms of examining their basic assumptions about their marriage, they might have stated them as follows:

Lois:

· *Marriage should be an exciting adventure with enough drama to keep it alive and interesting.*

· *Marriage should be a partnership of two people who share similar values with regard to their marriage and parenting.*

· *I feel good about whom I've become since divorcing Barry, and*

I'm sure that Eric will fulfill my needs for a husband to share my life.

· *I believe that Eric will do his best to provide for us, and I want to be a full partner with him in that.*

· *Eric will make a fine stepfather to my three children and a good father for our baby, should we have another child.*

Eric:

· *I wasn't ready for my marriages to Estelle and Maggie, but I'm much more settled now, and I'm ready for a responsible life with Lois.*

· *I want to experience being a father. I like Lois's kids, and I look forward to being a stepfather to them. If Lois and I can have a child of our own, that would be great.*

· *While my lust for adventuring has subsided, it hasn't disappeared by any means, and I look forward to having a partner with whom I can share my adventures. I see Lois as such a partner.*

· *I am a bit concerned about providing for Lois and my new family. I know I can always get a job, but it's time I pull all my skills together and build a career that provides a better income and more security for us all. I am quite sure that Lois will be supportive and will want to be involved any way she can.*

Assessment and predictions

There is much compatibility between Lois and Eric's assumptions as they enter their marriage. One can predict that, with a willingness on their parts to make appropriate adjustments, they should do just fine. Fortunately for them, the turmoil and ravaging of Eric's midlife crisis seem to have produced revised assumptions that are much more predictive of marital stability than his earlier ones.

And Lois may have found a more suitable match than before for her dramatic flair.

With regard to parenting issues—given that Lois's three children are well on their way to adulthood, and their father,

Barry, continues to actively parent the three of them—Lois and Eric appear to be in good shape, despite Eric's lack of parenting experience. Eric and Lois's assumptions about involving him as a stepfather to them could prove problematic, depending on the needs and wishes of everyone involved.

And one can only ponder the impact on their marriage should Eric's wish to have his vasectomy reversed be granted. The Fairy Godfather in charge of such things may be curious enough about how this adventurous pair will deal with such a birthing to grant Eric's wish.

Late-Adult Marriages

Every age deals with special challenges, some of them unique. Surviving into one's senior years brings one face to face with questions of how best to deal with life's late afternoon and evening years. Entering into marriage at this stage means daring to walk the remaining miles hand in hand with a partner. Many potential benefits attach to late-adult marriages that offer protection against the dread forces of the night: companionship, security, shared pleasures, financial advantage, avoiding the scourge of loneliness. But there is also another potential benefit that might be overlooked: the opportunity to reexamine what marriage can mean to you and your spouse and discover new ways to express the hopes and dreams that can yet flourish within you.

The bottom line is: *How we think about our aging shapes what we will be doing with it.*

If we choose passive survival for our remaining years, that's what we will bring into our lives. If we choose active growth and meaningful (to us) projects, we will create our lives accordingly. Or, to quote one of our greatest sages: *It ain't over 'til it's over.*

Too many of us live our golden years as if we have already reached our final resting place and there's little left for us to do. We might do better to believe that our life is *never* over and to use this assumption to shape our senior citizenship. And the same can be said of the assumptions we bring to our late-adult marriage. We do not have to bring the same old assumptions into this marriage. We don't have to live out once more the scripts of our younger years. We can create new scenarios with fresh vistas and goals more relevant to who we are now and who we want to become in the futures that remain to us.

Vince and Nora

Nora:

It seemed almost beyond comprehension to Nora that, in her 64th year, she would say "Yes" to Vince's latest in his series of pro-posals of marriage. After all, she had had 18 years of freedom from the second of her two seriously flawed marriages. Well, she thought, they weren't total disasters: she had three daughters and two sons and nine grandchildren. But both husbands had been abusive, hardening her against marrying again. Besides, she had grown much stronger and independent with the challenges and rewards of surviving and providing as a single parent. And why, for heaven's sake, should she choose this particular time—in her second year of retirement after 18 years of hard labor with the Family Services Agency—to risk marrying again?

And yet she and Vince had been living together for the past six years, and she had never known a kinder, more considerate man than he. Unlike both her exes, Vince listened attentively, engaged her as an equal, and had never behaved abusively. Despite her bone-deep distrust of men, she had come to feel more safe with Vince than with any man she had ever known. From this sense of safety she found herself loving Vince differently from the way she had ever loved another man, and found herself—much to her sur-prise—agreeing to marry him.

Clearly, Nora's powerful assumption that husbands are a bur-den and not to be trusted was bumping up against a fresh, newer assumption that Vince would be a different sort of husband.

Nora, in her weighing of the merits of marrying Vince, seems typical. Why on earth should she trade her security as a single woman for the uncertainties of a third marriage, this time to a 75-year-old man whom she will probably outlive and have to take care of before too much longer? The answer—if she is to say "yes"—must come from deep inside her self-awareness, or surely it is an act of folly. If all behavior is purposeful, this act must have a purpose somewhere in her awareness.

Nora's purpose is the same one that motivates all of us: to grow ourselves as we best understand. Despite her doubts and fears, Nora at age 64 is committing herself to what she assumes will result in her further growth. She is betting that being married to Vince will yield more growth than not.

And what about Vince?

Vince:

Vince, like Nora, also survived two earlier marriages, both ending in divorce. Fifteen years have passed since his last divorce, and now, at 75, he is overjoyed at the prospect of transforming his and Nora's six-year relationship into a legal marriage. As he laughingly confesses to Nora, he relishes the chance to once again marry a younger woman. But Nora and all of their friends regard Vince as much younger than his age, both physically and mentally. Active and alert, he views his retirement from his years as a school psychologist as an opportunity to create a new career for himself as a writer.

Vince sees his and Nora's marriage more as a God-given opportunity and a wonderful challenge than an insurance policy against living and dying alone. He is aware that, as a rule, older single men don't thrive. He knows that suicide rates among older single men are four times higher than for older married men, and the incidence of death from stroke and heart disease is much higher than that. So his decision to marry again and to marry Nora, if she will have him, comes for him more easily than it does for her.

But he is also aware that the quality of the rest of his life depends on his commitment to keep on growing as if he were ageless.

A

At 75, Vince is aware of his basic assumptions regarding his own personal growth and marriage.

Assumptions that are driving Vince's behavior:
· His thriving requires that he continue to generate and pit himself against meaningful challenges. Without such challenges, he will, to all intents and purposes, die. And he intends to live.
· Marrying Nora is his best bet. It will challenge both of them to build a productive and pleasurable life together.
· He understands Nora well enough to see clearly the major challenge that faces them: creating a marriage that defies Nora's deeply rooted expectation that this, like all her marriages, is doomed to failure.
· This marriage will prove different from Nora's previous ones only if it is nonabusive and nonadversarial. If this marriage reduces itself to a power struggle, it will reinforce her negative assumptions. But if it can be shaped into a safe and nurturing environment, Nora's potential to grow beyond her old boundaries can be unleashed, and this marriage will be different. He assumes that Nora has the potential to stretch well beyond her current self, and he is intrigued and curious to see what choices she will make, given the opportunity.
· Vince sees in Nora a beautiful and powerful woman and a fitting and appropriate mate and partner for the life he is committed to pursue in the years remaining to him. He regards himself as extremely fortunate that his previous marriages were also to beautiful, strong women. He thrived in both marriages and owes them both a profound debt—his life, really. Now, with Nora, he has another chance to do even better, a chance he will not pass up.

Assessment and predictions

For Vince and Nora, achieving a happy, thriving marriage depends on how well Vince lives out his intentions, as expressed in his assumptions, and on Nora's resiliency. If Nora's pessimistic assumptions born of her previous marriages catch up with and overwhelm her positive hopes for this one, she may well choose to scuttle this voyage with Vince. If Vince can sustain the safe, loving marriage that Nora needs to allow herself to let go of her reservations, she may well choose to fully engage herself in this one. Liberating oneself from the agonies and limitations of negative assumptions frees one to embrace a fresh and creative future.

How long will it take for Nora to be able to let go of the old and embrace the new?

Will Vince and Nora successfully avoid or neutralize the hot-button situations likely to rekindle Nora's fears that this marriage, too, will be a repeat of her past ones?

Will they make it to the promised land of marital bliss and dwell therein forever and ever?

One never knows for sure, but for Nora and Vince the odds are good.

No Simple Answers

We like to find easy answers and explanations for why a marriage fails: *He was an alcoholic. She cheated on me.* Whatever the simple answer, it can never take into account the factors and variables that interact with each other in the complex experience we call marriage.

In some cultures, as in our own in former times, husbands and wives lived out the days of their marriages in response to constraining rules and regulations reinforced by culture, religion and tradition. The options were few, particularly for wives, and the penalties for violating marital norms were greater than they are now. In such circumstances, the complexities of marriage tend to be contained and controlled, and marital discord, rather than appearing as a problem to be solved, becomes an embarrassment to be concealed from the neighbors.

From our current vantage point, life and marriage appear to have been simpler back then. Today, norms are more relaxed, rules and regulations are less punitive, and individual freedom of action is broader, again particularly for women. Today's freer environment and the fascinating complexity of each one of us make simple explanations for the failures and successes of any marriage difficult to come by. Should we come up with a simple explanation, we are likely to find that it blocks rather than encourages our deeper understanding of what really happened.

By discovering and understanding the roles our assumptions play in shaping our marriages, we take a giant step toward understanding the complexity of our lives in the real world.

WHAT TO DO ABOUT THEM

1. With regard to your views about marriage in general:
   · *What assumptions do you hold about marriage in general?*
   · *Which of your assumptions are optimistic? Which pessimistic?*

2. With regard to your views about your own marriage:
   · *What assumptions are you making about your marriage in particular?*
   · *How did you come by your assumptions?*
   · *From whom and where did you acquire them?*
   · *Who are your particular role models for how to do marriage?*

3. About the assumptions of your partner concerning marriage:
   · *What do you know about your partner's assumptions concerning your marriage?*
   · *How certain are you about this knowledge of yours?*
   · *Do the two of you discuss with each other your respective assumptions about marriage? Ever? Sometimes? Often?*

Notes & Comments

Notes & Comments

6

Assumptions About Aging

Topic Index

6
Assumptions About Aging

For all of us, young and old, our assumptions about aging have profound impact. We age more rapidly, give up more easily, and die sooner if we cling to assumptions that declare, in one way or another: *The end is near, so what's the use!* If, on the other hand, we adopt assumptions that declare, in effect: *Every day opens new adventures and unexplored opportunities!* we invigorate our lives with renewed energy and exciting creativity. It is important to understand that this deep chasm between basic pessimism and basic optimism about our aging is bridgeable. And all it takes is enough information and intent to transform our negative assumptions about growing older into positive ones.

This chapter is designed to help you accomplish just that.

Who Better?

If you qualify for AARP membership, you are an authority on aging to some extent. Simply by surviving all those years in life's school of hard knocks, you have been promoted to the Senior class, whether you wished to be or not. If for no other reason, I can therefore rightfully proclaim myself to be this book's *Resident Guru on Aging*. For, as you read this, I am either anticipating my 80th birthday or remembering what a great party it was.

Frankly, I find it unbelievable that I am or soon will become an *octogenarian!* I'm surprised that I've made it this far. But since I have, I am anticipating the next phase of my life with excitement and optimism. I am also aware that my body's biological clock—

to say nothing of drunk drivers and other impediments—may not grant me the time to do all the things I am eager to do. We all live only in this moment, with an anticipation of more that may not be fulfilled. The awareness pushes me to make the most of what I am given.

So what does the resident guru at his four-score milepost have to say on the subject of assumptions about aging?

I can begin by identifying and commenting on the particular assumptions of mine that I regard as enhancing healthy aging and, conversely, those contrasting assumptions that I regard as inhibiting healthy aging. I find that all of these assumptions affect the quality as well as the quantity of my life.

As a general rule, negative assumptions contribute to bodily illness—such as cancer, stroke, high blood pressure—as well as to making one's aging a miserable and bitter experience. Positive assumptions contribute to physical, emotional and spiritual well-being—vital ingredients of quality aging.

Assumptions About Aging That Work for Me

Following are nine assumptions about aging that work for me. In each case the word (or words) identifying the assumption's central concern is offered in opposition to its negative counterpart, followed by a description of the assumption. For example, assumption #1 addresses my own concern around living in fear as opposed to living in a state of fearlessness.

1. Fearless v. fearful

Assumption: *Living in fear is not conducive to healthy aging. Living without fear is.*

I have lived in fear enough already! I have learned the lesson that until you confront and deal with the sources of your fear, it clutches you in its grip as surely as the spider clutches the fly. The fly may not escape, but we can if we seek the sources of our fears that lie locked in the mind and transcend or rework them. In the end, we must let go of our fear or carry it with us cancerlike to our death. Not an easy task but doable, given time and intent.

I can say that for now I live fear-free, and have for the past year and more. To achieve this state has been worth the years it has taken. My own experiences with fear, at least since World War II, have rarely been of the life-threatening kind—mostly fears of inadequacy, rejection, abandonment, failure, disgrace, the usual mundane stuff that infests most of our lives, like fungus and worms. But mundane or not, these are fears that take longest and are hardest to overcome because their roots lie tangled and often deeply hidden in our personal histories.

For me, back there in midlife, it was the yearning for disentanglement that drove me to choose a career as a psychotherapist. And the joy and excitement of discovery that disentanglement brings with it has driven my life ever since.

2. Flexible, resilient v. rigid

Assumption: *Being flexible and resilient is more conducive to healthy aging than being rigid.*

We seniors are particularly challenged by the magnitude and number of changes taking place over the course of our lifetimes. No past generations of elders have had to adapt as much or as fast just to keep up. Whether we wished to or not, we have spent a lifetime snakelike: shedding old skins of understanding and behavior and growing new ones as each new adaptation requires. To survive and flourish in this time of millennium demands flexibility and resilience of everyone, of every age. Opportunities to learn new skills and discover new paths have never been more available for oldsters.

However, there is a particularly vital way to use our flexibility and resiliency: We all know the powerful urge to get even for past violations, to want revenge for past wounds, to right the scales for having been unjustly treated. Some of us go to our graves holding on to our righteous indignation—and we probably get there sooner and enjoy living less because of it. By not letting go of our hunger to avenge past hurts and by clinging to our suffering, we pour our emotional energy—our power—into prolonging unwinnable wars against imagined enemies. Inflexibly clinging to hope of final victory is self-defeating. In the end, we lose the option of using our emotional energy in more life-giving ways. We lose the flexibility and freedom of letting go and releasing. We lose the joy and excitement of renewal. We lose the opportunity to enjoy healthy aging.

3. Accepting v. rejecting, denying

Assumption: *Accepting all that life hands out to us offers more advantages and opportunities than denying or rejecting.*

I use *accepting* to mean *acknowledging the existence of,* not necessarily *to do nothing.*

Just as our addictions are untreatable so long as we deny their existence, acceptance is prerequisite to our dealing effectively with whatever situation we are responding to with denial. By accepting, we open up possibilities for actively responding in whatever way we choose. We can even choose to do nothing about our situation, and such a choice is always an option. But as with every other choice, we at least acknowledge the existence of our situation as opposed to turning a blind eye. Choosing to continue smoking while accepting that we are indeed addicted is a healthier choice, at least psychologically, than denying our addiction.

Our lives and our health are always at risk. Denial increases the odds of being blindsided by perils whose existence we are choosing not to acknowledge. Denial may safeguard our comforting rationalizations for a time, but it ups the ante by increasing the risk.

Life-threatening addictions—particularly to alcohol and tobacco—
are better caught sooner than later.

4. Forgiving v. not forgiving

Assumption: *Forgiving those who trespass against us is better for
healthy aging than not forgiving.*

A friend of mine told about the project his Sunday School
class of about a dozen boys and girls had undertaken. Working
with scissors, paste and old magazines, they created a collage of
words and pictures they thought would help build a peaceful world
populated with more decent people. Among the words the children selected was *forgiving.*

From the mouths of babes!

Forgiving impacts the forgiver as much or more than the for-
given because of its power to release. By letting go of the anger and
resentment that energizes our refusal to forgive, we free our emotional energy to flow in healthier and more loving ways. The wellness
and good will that attach to our acts of forgiving are vital to our
healthy aging.

Moreover, refusing to forgive is a wasteful distraction. Instead
of paying attention to our growth needs and enjoying our lives, we
distract ourselves with niggle-nagging bitterness and resentment.
Instead of enjoying the company of others, we distract ourselves
by measuring their shortcomings and counting their sins.

But forgiving others is only half the battle for healthy aging;
forgiving yourself is the other half. The elderly often rue so many
of their choices and paths not taken over the years, and in being so
preoccupied with self-castigation, they obliterate all the possibilities that may be there for them in the present.

5. Loving v. hating

Assumption: *Loving is a whole lot healthier for us than hating, regardless of age.*

It really is possible for us to replace all of our hating with loving. Loving our enemies is as simple as letting go of the word *enemy* and replacing it with *friend,* or *sister,* or *brother,* or *someone who could be me.* Walking in another's shoes is to experience them as if we are they. Allow ourselves that experience, and we open the door to loving rather than hating.

Why is loving healthier for us than hating?

As mind-body organisms, our psychological states greatly influence our mental and physical health.

As anyone who experienced the sixties may remember, loving is a more opening experience than hating. Loving opens us up, expanding our senses and sensibilities. Conversely, hating constricts and shuts us down. We see fewer options in a state of hate, and all of them do violence of one sort or another. In a loving state we see many possibilities, and all of them are of peaceful intent.

For all of these reasons (or assumptions, if you prefer), as well as my own life experiences, I am drawn to conclude that a loving environment is much more conducive to healthy growth than a hateful one.

6. Playful, youthful, childlike v. denying inner impulses

Assumption: *Being young in mind and heart, if not in body, is productive of healthy aging. Rejecting our inner potential for youthfulness is counterproductive.*

Aging need not be taken seriously. It really can be a fun time for all. Your grandkids love playful grandmas and grandpas, and to deny them and you that experience is both sad and wasteful. The same goes for other situations where you dismiss your more playful impulses because some parental voice in your mind is telling you to *Act Your Age!*

Parental voices aside, acting your age means allowing your natural goodness to come out and express itself in ways that enliven you. Your inner child is as full of health and vigor as you will allow. Release your childlike self. It may well bring you a wonderful sense of renewal, allowing the expression of the valid and valuable aspects of who you are. And your natural gifts for spontaneity and optimism will create many joyful moments and improve the quality of your days.

7. *Purposeful* v. purposeless, without purpose

Assumption: *Living a purposeful life is healthy for older people too.*

All it takes to live the purposeful life is to be aware of one's options and to make conscious choices among them. Purposefulness—being full of a sense of purpose to one's life—is not a natural choice for seniors in our culture. The culture's emphasis on youth has marginalized aging as an awkward and embarrassing inconvenience that befalls those who survive beyond the "normal" limits of adulthood. Consequently, most of us were not schooled to consider our later years as a time for renewal and fulfillment of life's purpose.

By and large, we have been a generation of seniors cut off from family and productive employment. The well-to-do among us have withdrawn to retirement communities extolling The Joy of Retirement and excluding children. We've taken to the road in pursuit of meaningful places and relief from our isolation, advertising our rage on bumper stickers that threaten to "get even" by spending our children's inheritance. Cut off from a functional place and role in our families, most of us drift through our later years feeling left out, diminished and bewildered too much for our own good.

It need not be so. You can change this scenario by living out the rest of your years consciously and conscientiously in pursuit of the purposes of your choice. It's not how grand and ambitious your choices are—it is delighting in your ability to create each new day and choose how to spend your next hour. You may choose to plan for and savor dinner—or make bigger choices like volunteering to make fund-raising calls for suicide prevention or tutoring or joining others in building a house for Habitat for Humanity or collecting stamps or launching a Web site.

How fortunate we are to have come into an age full of opportunities for us—and our children—to reassess and revise the role of elders in our culture.

8. Active v. passive

Assumption: *Active living makes for healthier and happier aging than passive existence.*

By *Active living,* I mean exercising and maintaining an active mind-body.

I love to walk and make a habit of walking daily. Mostly, I love to walk beaches. For the past 40 years I have been choosing to live either at the ocean's edge or within commuting distance so I can indulge my love for beachwalking.

I'm a lover of birds, and I love watching the gulls and pelicans swoop and dive, and the sanderlings scurrying behind the surf, halting to dip a beak and pluck a morsel before scurrying on, or swooping away down the beach in a swirling flock. Often I walk with my eyes closed for long periods, guided by the sound of surf on one side, the texture of sand underfoot, the direction of wind on my face, trusting my sightless senses to save me from wandering into the sea.

But I love beachwalking most when I'm combining my physical experience with problem solving. I have heaps of memories of my beachwalks over the years. I can recall most of the major transitions in my life by the particular walks on which I grappled with the problems they posed.

It's certainly important to my healthy aging that I have chosen a new career with no time limits and over which I have complete control. I can attend to my writing under most any and all circumstances, and much of it happens while walking. That is where my books are usually flamed into life and shaped and developed. That's where the next steps and writing blocks are usually addressed and resolved.

It's neither by neglect nor accident that in my eighties I have more books to write and publish beyond this one. I am choosing a schedule of activity designed to carry me to the outer limits of my life. I plan to die within a last gasp of completing my last book. And I hope to be still ambulatory on the day before I pass. That would make me happy.

It's this combination of walking and pondering that I find most satisfying. That's my favorite mind-body exercise.

What is yours?

9. Considering, reflective v. inattentive, unthinking

Assumption: *Considering and reflecting are conducive to healthy aging.*

Much as the Goddess of Wisdom lavishes her gifts on the elderly, you are not going to get wise just because you get old. Wisdom rises to the surface of the mind naturally, like cream. If you allow your mind to stagnate, you'll get sour milk. But attend it with consideration and keep it stirring, and you'll discover the globules of golden butter that light up and enrich your aging with wisdom.

I won't debate the question, *What is wisdom?* In my experience, one person's wisdom is another's drivel. The important question to consider is, *What is your wisdom?* And your wisdom is the pure essence yielded up by your life. What pearls has your life led you to? And if you haven't discovered any as yet, what might you do to earn for yourself that pleasure?

Choosing to be reflective—allowing yourself to reflect, since it comes naturally with aging—is prerequisite. Gently squeezing your mind with questions that encourage you to think about your own life more deeply can illuminate your understanding with fresh insights.

There is no shortage of wisdom out there for you to consider. We are being assaulted from all sides by pundits. Listening to the pundits of your choice and considering what they have to offer can help point the way to the wisdom. Swallowing theirs whole won't. Considering theirs can. It's the process of considering, reflecting upon, weighing, evaluating, through which you will come to yours. It's the digesting that yields your pearls, not the swallowing.

Living to Ripeness Before Falling Off the Tree

Never before have we seniors had so much opportunity to commit the rest of our lives to whatever purposes we choose. Whatever our dreams for personal fulfillment, we live at a time when almost all things are possible. Only our assumptions regarding *What's possible?* set the limits to what we will reach for.

Want to go to college and get that degree? Sail the South Pacific and live on a small island? Move to Florida and bask in the sunshine? Join the Peace Corps? Write a novel?

What unfulfilled dreams do you have, and what are you doing about them? Are you hiding your dreams in a closet, not daring to bring them into the reality of your daily life? Are you assuming you can't possibly try to fulfill them?

John Glenn's dream of a geriatric return to space could never have been fulfilled had he not assumed he could do it.

Neil Van Steenbergen climbed Mt. Kilimanjaro at age 70 and now, at age 73, is spending the year 2000 bicycling around the world. Without the assumption that such adventures are possible, his dreams would go unfulfilled for lack of trying.

How many seniors do you know who are devoting their postretirement years to making fresh starts in new directions?

Are you one of them? If not, what assumptions are you making that are getting in your way?

The Prospect of Graduating from the Karmic Wheel

The assumption that there is a God is an acknowledgement of your spiritual connection to that which transcends your physical earthly existence. If you are a believer, you also are assuming you are endowed with a spiritual as well as a physical nature. But even if you are a nonbeliever, your awareness of your own mortality may lead you to embrace the assumption that you are more than a physical being. The knowledge (assumption) that everyone dies begs the question, *What will happen after my death?* And the question may lead you to ponder the nature and meaning of your connection to some larger and more abiding context. Until we experience our own death, we have no alternative but to take all our assumptions about the hereafter as a matter of faith.

Quality aging means living up to our human potential as we ourselves best judge. That surely includes attending to our spiritual growth and development. Aging offers every one of us the luxury to attend to—and enjoy—the spiritual dimensions of our lives. Social Security and Medicare give us disposable time we can use for spiritual awakening and spiritual growth. And the aging process itself pushes us to address such questions as,

What is the purpose and meaning of my life? What have I accomplished with this life that was granted me? What have I left undone? What can I still do that has meaning for me?

While we often ask such questions in our earlier years, aging gives them greater weight and urgency.

Given the predictions in this time of the millennium of an exploding population of seniors, I am fascinated by the prospect of millions of baby boomers about to come into their maturity, all asking questions that plumb their spiritual depths. I can imagine the rumbling of their many voices resounding across the length and breadth of our civilization, raising spiritual awareness to new levels. I look for great changes to result. I plan to live long enough to witness them.

Two Typical Problems of Aging

Retirement, particularly for men of my generation, can bring with it the loss of the major social role and identity—worker, bread-winner, productive team member—that gave positive meaning to life. The loss of job and the social identity that attaches to it can drown anticipations of joyful retirement with a depressing flood of sadness, purposelessness, impotence and grief. Where such depression persists without effective treatment, suicide and other forms of induced premature death often follow.

1. Time on my hands

Having an abundance of time on our hands always requires us to decide what to do with it. Even choosing to do nothing about it is a decision. And all our decisions derive from particular assumptions that reflect our wants, fears, dreams, longings, entitlements, missions, and obligations. So long as our assumptions open us up to considering them, our choices for how to use our abundance of time are limitless.

I've always longed for the time when I didn't have to do anything but loaf, and by God I'm going to spend the rest of my life doing just that!

I want to become a nun (or priest) and devote the rest of my life to doing God's work.

I want to throw a javelin in the Senior Olympics.

I want to become a wise investor in the stock market from my home computer.

I want to travel the world and learn about foreign places and cultures.

I want to sit in cozy corners and read books.

Perhaps for the first time in your life you find yourself in a position where you can use your time in whatever manner you choose. Ask yourself if you are choosing well. And if not, what assumptions are you making that keep you from doing so?

2. www.aging.com

Aging in the age of the Internet can be as full of opportunities and challenges as you wish it to be. Only your negative assumption that you can't possibly learn to use a computer stands in your way.

Accessing the Web gets easier all the time. If you can type your name on a keyboard, you're halfway there. Taking a class in computer basics at your local community college or senior center can put you on-line where you can expand your options and explore your possibilities. And it's wonderfully satisfying to realize that you really can learn to do this stuff.

If you're not on-line with your e-mail address, you're missing out. E-mail is great for keeping in touch with far-flung kids and friends. They are never more than a few mouse clicks away, even if you are in San Francisco and they are on the other side of the world. And the Internet gives you fingertip access to whatever you wish to learn, explore and do.

Of course, none of us can keep pace with *all* the technological changes happening, but you don't have to. You don't have to travel first-class to keep up with your fellow passengers on the 21st Century Limited. Most of us don't care whether our computer is a 6,000 megabyte SuperDuper Deluxe or an old-fashioned Macintosh. Either one serves the purpose for most of our needs.

The most important advantage of becoming computer literate is that it gives you tremendous control over your life. You are completely in charge of what you do with your computer. Want to write your memoirs? Find out stuff without having to go to your local library? Complain to your congressional representative? Post your favorite recipes on your own Web site? Think of your computer as a cornucopia of gifts designed to make your remaining years truly golden.

Your assumption that you can't possibly learn to use a computer is the only impediment that puts this cornucopia beyond your reach.

Contrasting Perceptions of Aging

Almost 20 years ago physicist and philosopher Fritjof Capra, in his book *The Turning Point* (Simon and Shuster, 1982), saw our current crisis of civilization as arising from our perceiving the world through the wrong model—or as I prefer to state, accepting outworn assumptions. In Capra's view we have been applying a mechanistic Cartesian-Newtonian model to a reality that can no longer be understood in such terms. Our future, Capra insisted, hinges on a shift to a Systems model, which emphasizes a view of all things as interacting and interdependent.

We have made considerable progress in shifting from a Cartesian-Newtonian to a Systems model in the last 20 years, particularly in our understanding of the universe and in the sciences. But Capra's call for us to make this shift applies as well to our understanding of ourselves. And in that, we have a long way to go.

Colin, Brad, and Leurice

Perhaps because Colin is an engineer, he finds it easy to think in terms of a Cartesian-Newtonian model when he talks about aging. He equates aging with an inevitable running down of the human machinery. Colin, who is in his mid-forties, says:

> When I think about aging, I think about the body getting older and losing some of its pizazz. I guess I'm speaking of degenerative aging. You're always aging, but up to about 30 you seem to be on the rise. Past 30 you seem to start declining in your physical abilities. In some sense your mental abilities start declining somewhat later than that—I think in the forties or fifties.
>
> I don't think anybody really likes to age. What bothers me more than the running down of the physical machine is the running down of the mental machine. I'm really resisting the running down of the mental machine. I'm fighting that.

In contrast to Colin's view of aging as a wearing down of both a physical machine and a mental machine, Brad, 32, an oceanographer, envisions a biological model of aging.

> You go through an initial period of rapid growth, and eventually you stop growing. I guess it's at that point that I see you as aging. That's partly because I grow cultures of plants, and they go through a period of growing real fast and then go into senescence. I think that's the model I have in mind. I'm talking physically.
>
> Mentally, I think aging can be growing wiser, or it can also be a downhill slide, with your body falling apart and your mind getting less sharp. Or it can also be honing your skills to a fine edge, and even improving your physical skills and agility.
>
> I guess to me, aging doesn't have anything to do with whether you're actually building your body and mind; it's simply the process of marking time after you stop going through that initial spurt of growth.

When we think of aging as the breaking down of our human machinery or as inevitable biological decline that follows an initial surge of growth, we are using assumptions that are characteristic of the Cartesian-Newtonian view. In that regard, both Colin and Brad are basing their assumptions of aging on a Cartesian-Newtonian model.

Leurice, retired from a nursing career at age 63, views aging with a more Systems-model approach.

> *Aging wasn't anything I looked forward to, but I knew it was going to happen. I just knew one grows old. I didn't fear it. I just hoped I'd be physically and mentally alert to the day I die.*
>
> *I didn't expect to be a widow, to have asthma, or to be living alone. And choices narrow down, like not being able to just walk out and get a job. As a nurse I never experienced a time when I couldn't go out and get a job.*

But Leurice's response to aging has been to counterattack rather than submit. While she accepts that her choices have narrowed in some dimensions, she has elaborated them in others.

> *I learned to knit. I went to yoga classes. I've taken classes with a practitioner of (Moshe) Feldenkrais. I've joined N.O.W. (National Organization for Women). I'm in a consciousness-raising group. I read more fully about politics and understand issues better. And I do some letter writing I thought I never had time for.*

Leurice's commitment to her continuing growth takes into account a keen awareness of her physical vulnerability. She reports she retired at 63 "out of necessity," shorthand for a variety of circumstances, including her developing a serious case of asthma and high blood pressure. Since then, she has worked hard to recover and maintain her physical well-being.

I felt the aging process more physically a few years ago than I do now. Asthma put limits on my endurance, but it's better than it was. And my blood pressure has started to level out this past year, and it's no longer at the danger point.

For Leurice, her improving physical condition has put to rest the idea that it's all necessarily downhill after 40 or 50 or 60. She credits her big turnaround to the Feldenkrais method.

The Feldenkrais class was a big turning point for me. He organizes the body and the mind to work together. The way we move is the way we think. The exercises are all done on the floor. They're not vigorous. Some of them are repetitive. You become very aware of what your body is doing, and you change your muscle patterns and your movement patterns. And it does change your mind patterns! It's really amazing.

Leurice has responded to her aging process with a Systems-model holistic philosophy. Her assertive stance toward life is the outer manifestation of an inner battle against an omnipresent specter. She is an excellent example of how we might best respond when disability strikes: Finding alternative ways to continue growing to replace those that have fallen by the wayside, and resisting our tendency to think of ourselves as inevitably declining toward death.

WHAT TO DO ABOUT THEM

The author lists nine assumptions about aging that he identifies as working for him. Which of the following assumptions also work for you? Which ones do not?

1. *Living in fear is not conducive to healthy aging. Living without fear is.*
2. *Being flexible and resilient is more conducive to healthy aging than being inflexible and rigid.*
3. *Accepting all that life hands out to us offers more advantages and opportunities than denying or rejecting.*
4. *Forgiving those who trespass against us is better for healthy aging than not forgiving.*
5. *Loving is a whole lot healthier for us than hating, regardless of age.*
6. *Being young in mind and heart, if not in body, is productive of healthy aging. Rejecting our inner potential for youthfulness is counterproductive.*
7. *Living a purposeful life is healthy for older people too.*
8. *Active living makes for healthier and happier aging than passive existence.*
9. *Considering and reflecting are conducive to healthy aging.*

Notes & Comments

Notes & Comments

Notes & Comments

7
Assumptions
About Death and Dying

Topic Index

7

Assumptions
About Death and Dying

Dying is the one act that brings the same physical outcome for every one of us. Each of us ends up dead. But the style and quality of our living and dying, as well as our anticipations and apprehensions around dying and afterlife, are shaped by our assumptions which, in turn, are reflective of our religious and spiritual orientations.

No doubt, the ultimate test of our assumptions about death and dying lies in how well they hold up in our own dying experience. But the following concerns are more important than how on target or wide of the mark our assumptions may prove to be:

How well are they working for us now?
Do they make living more rewarding and satisfying?
Do they promise to make our own dying experience more growth-enhancing and more fulfilling? Or less?

All of life is learning time. This is as true for our last days as for our first. Each day, first and last, offers the potential to learn and grow. Whether it is easier or more difficult to learn and grow in the earlier stages of life than in the final ones is irrelevant. What is relevant is the choice we make to participate actively in our learning and growing process.

About this Chapter

I begin this chapter by sharing with you my own assumptions around death and dying together with a little background to explain, in part, how I came by them. The chapter then looks at a host of assumptions expressed by Elizabeth Kübler-Ross, M.D., whose pioneering research in the dying process has led her profession and the rest of us to a more compassionate and humane understanding of what it means to die. Quality of Life and Right to Die issues are discussed in the later sections of the chapter, and the *What to do about them* exercise asks you to explore your own assumptions around death and dying by comparing them to those expressed by Kübler-Ross.

My Assumptions and How I Came by Them

The core assumptions that drive my own beliefs and behaviors about dying and death were not taught to me in childhood. What I did learn as a child came primarily from two sources: my parents and my first nine years of living in a small New Jersey community named in memory of a Spanish educator, Francisco Ferrer.

An anarchist and fiercely anticlerical, Ferrer believed in education free from the authority of church and state. He was executed in 1909 for establishing—in defiance of the Catholic Church—the *Escuela Moderna,* a "Modern" or libertarian school in Barcelona, Spain. My first four years of schooling took place at the Modern School at Stelton, New Jersey, patterned after Ferrer's *Escuela Moderna.*

My father and mother, Misha Bogart and Emma Baskin, were both Russian Jews who came to this country among the masses of Eastern European immigrants fleeing to the New World in the years before World War I. By the time I came into the world in 1921, they had found each other, married, produced my older brother and, some short time after I was born, divorced.

I have no early memory of living with either parent. I remember that my older brother was a live-in student at the Modern School and that I lived a few miles away in the good care of a family that included two teenage children. I remember my mother in her nurse's uniform at Beth David Hospital in New York City. And I have memories of the happy company of cats and chickens, the piano and violin playing of the teenagers, occasional visits of my mother and frequent nightmares and bed wettings. Around the time I was five, my mother met and married Bernard Shane, who also travelled from Manhattan on weekends to visit his two children from a previous marriage. Sometime in 1926 we all came together as a new family, and I began attending the Modern School.

Of my earliest schooldays, I remember unlimited freedom to learn and do pretty much as we wished. I have no memories of classrooms or forced instruction and lots of memories of shared activities with other children: spending time in the library, writing poems and hand-setting them in type, running a pedal-operated printing press, building canoes of lathes and canvas and paddling them about in the pond, playing soccer, and all of us swimming naked.

In 1930 we moved to Chicago's north side and I traded in my Modern School freedom for Mrs. Charbonneau's fifth-grade class at the Eugene Field Elementary School. But I have fond memories of swimming in Lake Michigan, participating in a boy's Midget Life Guard program at the Touey Avenue Beach, and attending the Chicago World's Fairs of 1933 and 1934.

It wasn't until 1934, when we moved to Montreal, Canada, that, for the first time, I became conscious of living in a world where religion mattered.

Although my parents identified themselves as Jews and actively participated in Jewish cultural and political life, they were also, in their time, radicals who rejected affiliation with established religions. Both the terms *atheist* and *agnostic* approximate their religious orientation, as does the phrase *secular Jew* as it is used in Israel today. As a consequence, religious instruction and practice were nonexistent in the home and school environments of my early and preadolescent years. I grew up with the belief that God is a figment of religious imagination, that life ends in death, and that there is no afterlife in heaven or hell.

My parents enrolled me at Montreal High School, a Protestant school, and I entered a strange new world peopled, for the most part, by Protestants and Catholics separated from each other by language, religion and other factors of which I was yet unaware. More important to me, it was a world in which Jews were actively discriminated against by both.

In this milieu I soon found my early core assumptions about religion assailed from all sides. In response, I took to experimenting with a variety of strategies to fit whatever situation I found myself in. For the most part, I settled into masking my Jewish identity wherever I felt that being a Jew was inconvenient, without ever resorting to the ultimate lie of denying it verbally. This awareness of challenge to my core assumptions around issues of religion and my inclination to experiment have endured to this day in one form and another.

And where am I after all my years of challenge and experimentation?

Well, one core assumption I now accept is the existence of God, but more as a universal or cosmic intelligence than an anthropomorphic deity. In the cosmos wherein my God does His/Her/Its *Thing,* all life forms are information gatherers for the God-Mind at work. In this conceptualization, each of us, in some manner, functions as a nerve ending of a universal intelligence whose master plan, if there is any, is unknown to us and can only be conjectured about.

This particular core assumption leads me to a clear sense of our human purpose: To do our best to advance the larger body of intelligence within which each of us constitutes a unique, if tiny, part.

And how do we do this? By accepting the life challenges that God—or the universe—places before us as best we can. By that measure, we are all worthy. None of us is a failure. Not to say that we have done as well as we might, but that we have done our best, whatever that may be. Not to say that we can't or won't do better, but that, so far, we've done whatever our best amounts to.

As for my assumptions about an afterlife, while I am not wholly convinced of its correctness, I find comfort in the Buddhist belief that this life is but one of many that our spirit or soul acquires and lives through on its path to Buddhahood. I like this assumption because it holds the promise of a spiritual perfectibility that most of us cannot achieve within the confines of a single life. While Christianity promises Heaven after a single lifetime to those who believe, it doesn't really demand much of one. By contrast, the belief that we each have the potential to evolve toward purity of spirit and perfect being-ness, and that we are destined to reincarnate until we get it right, appeals to my Capricornian nature.

Elizabeth Kübler-Ross

Although I practiced as a social worker and psychotherapist for 25 years, I never specialized in working with the terminally ill. Nevertheless, Elizabeth Kübler-Ross, M.D., has always been my primary source of knowledge and inspiration about the process and meaning of death and dying. Although I never met her or attended her seminars and workshops, her classic study, *On Death and Dying*, was my principal guide to an understanding of the dying process.

So when it came time to write this chapter, I found myself asking, *What core assumptions about death and dying would Elizabeth Kübler-Ross be making?* And to find out, I turned to *The Wheel of Life: A Memoir of Living and Dying*, her latest and, as she states, "what is certain to be my final book."

I found *The Wheel of Life* an inspiring account of how her own core beliefs about God, life, death, dying, afterlife, and rebirth evolved over her years of working with many thousands of people facing their own "final graduation." This is one book I recommend if you are at all uncomfortable with your current assumptions about dying and death.

With regard to her own basic assumptions, Dr. Kübler Ross makes them readily identifiable at the very end of her book, where she offers a listing of her beliefs. Here they are (bullets added):

·   *All people come from the same source and return to the same source.*

·   *We must all learn to love and be loved unconditionally.*

·   *All the hardships that come to you in life, all the tribulations and nightmares, all the things you see as punishments from God, are in reality like gifts. They are an opportunity to grow, which is the sole purpose of life.*

·   *You cannot heal the world without healing yourself first.*

·   *If you are ready for spiritual experiences and you are not afraid, you will have them yourself. You do not need a guru or a Baba to tell you how to do it.*

·   *All of us, when we were born from the source, which I call God, were endowed with a facet of divinity. That is what gives us knowledge of our immortality.*

·   *You should live until you die.*

·   *No one dies alone.*

·   *Everyone is loved beyond comprehension.*

·   *Everyone is blessed and guided.*

·   *It is very important that you do only what you love to do. You may be poor, you may go hungry, you may live in a shabby place, but you will totally live. And at the end of your days, you will bless your life because you have done what you came here to do.*

·   *The hardest lesson to learn is unconditional love.*

·   *Dying is nothing to fear. It can be the most wonderful experience of your life. It all depends on how you have lived.*

·   *Death is but a transition from this life to another existence where there is no more pain and anguish.*

·   *Everything is bearable when there is love.*

·   *The only thing that lives forever is love.*

Dr. Kübler-Ross arrived at her assumptions over a professional lifetime of consciously pursuing a deep and detailed understanding of what it means to die. Few of us—and I am certainly not among them—pay that much attention to acquiring such understanding. Most of us are amateurs by comparison. Nevertheless, we are all profoundly shaped by our beliefs and attitudes having to do with death and dying.

Dying as Walking a Spiritual Path

Dr. Kübler-Ross speaks of dying well as a profound learning experience and final graduation. Her skill and compassion have helped many walk through that graduation ceremony with dignity and joy, and have taught many others how to be of service to the dying. I'm sure the same can be said of other spiritual leaders to whom is given a deeper understanding of life and death. So we all can seek models and teachers to whom we can turn for wisdom and guidance. But in the end, it is we—each of us—who will walk the walk.

A friend of mine has shared with me her experience of her father's dying. She said that she had not thought of him as a man who was particularly knowledgeable or sophisticated about spiritual matters, so she was completely surprised by the transformation he experienced in his final days and hours. She speaks of his *achieving his spiritual maturity, his Buddha nature* during his last days. She speaks of them as having been for him *a time of enlightenment and deep satisfaction.*

I call that a good dying. May it happen to all of us, and I think it can if we can sidestep or resolve the pain and fear of our negative thinking.

Preparing for one's death can be a time for drawing to closure all of one's life issues that continue to manifest. Whether closure comes through resolving one's issues, accepting that they are beyond one's ability to resolve, or transcending to a higher plateau

where they no longer have meaning or relevance, closure allows us
to open up to our true spiritual being.

I believe that our core constructs, our deepest beliefs, will de-
termine the manner and style with which we greet death. But I
also believe that regardless of our constructs, we are going to be
surprised by what we finally perceive to be the truth of the matter.
Hopefully, the surprise will come as a pleasant relief after all our
anxieties and concerns surrounding our dying.

If it isn't, ask for a refund.

The Right to Die with Dignity

Or, *Who gets to pull the plug?*

The major argument for assisted suicide is rooted in Quality
of Life issues. If suffering and pain diminish the quality of life
below some acceptable threshold, the argument goes, then assist-
ing the sufferer to end his or her life, if he or she so chooses, is
humane and justifiable. A counter argument, which Kübler-Ross
accepts, is that *We should live until we die.*

I admit to being something of a mugwump on the issue of
assisted suicide, straddling it with my mug on one side of the
fence and my wump on the other. Still, I know how I would have
things be in my Ideal World: We should each be granted the right
to choose our own path out of this mortal coil, whatever that path
may be. And we should each be supported and assisted in our
choice by whatever means are available.

To die in peace and dignity surrounded by family and friends
sounds to me like a lovely exit. To pass in this way serves as confir-
mation of one's life and as fitting ceremony for one's final graduation. When, for whatever reason, that is not allowed to happen,
those who remain among the living are left to grapple with the
aura of dissonance and unfinished-ness that hangs in the air. Instead of memories of a life lived well and fully, lamentations of
remorse and sadness, often tinged with guilt, can endure for years
in the minds of the survivors.

So the manner in which one dies has tremendous import for those who go on living. The benediction, *He died a hero's death,* may not be of enduring consequence to the deceased, but it certainly impacts the survivors. Of such stuff are our mythologies (our core assumptions) woven into the fabric of our thoughts and memories. We all live with the consequences of death—the remainders as well as the reminders.

It would be so much easier on the living if everyone were to die happy deaths. But, as the saying goes, *Nobody said it would be easy.*

WHAT TO DO ABOUT THEM

To help you clarify your own assumptions around issues of death and dying, take the time to think about which of the following beliefs expressed by Elizabeth Kübler-Ross you agree or disagree with.

- *All people come from the same source and return to the same source.*
- *All the hardships that come to you in life, all the tribulations and nightmares, all the things you see as punishments from God, are in reality like gifts. They are an opportunity to grow, which is the sole purpose of life.*
- *You cannot heal the world without healing yourself first.*
- *If you are ready for spiritual experiences and you are not afraid, you will have them yourself. You do not need a guru or a Baba to tell you how to do it.*
- *All of us, when we were born from the source, which I call God, were endowed with a facet of divinity. That is what gives us knowledge of our immortality.*
- *You should live until you die.*
- *No one dies alone.*
- *The hardest lesson to learn is unconditional love.*
- *Dying is nothing to fear. It can be the most wonderful experience of your life. It all depends on how you have lived.*
- *Death is but a transition from this life to another existence where there is no more pain and anguish.*
- *The only thing that lives forever is love.*

Notes & Comments

Notes & Comments

Notes & Comments

8

CONVERSATIONS

Four Highly Effective People Talk

About Assumptions That Work for Them

Topic Index

8

CONVERSATIONS

Four Highly Effective People Talk

About Assumptions That Work for Them

In the four chapters that follow, we shift to a different style and form of presentation as we explore with four recognized experts assumptions that make the difference between success and failure in their respective occupations.

My conversations with each of them are presented in interview form, very much but not exactly as they were recorded on audiotape. Transcripts of recorded interviews were edited and reviewed by the interviewee to make sure he or she was not being misquoted or misrepresented in any way. Basically, you get to share the essence of what our experts had to say in their own words.

In the chapters that follow, we explore with our guests the particular assumptions that guide them in their chosen fields. Two of them are highly effective leaders in their fields of childhood development and remedial education. The third is a nationally recognized executive officer for a leading high tech corporation. And the fourth is a successful small-business entrepreneur who is also an award-winning author, documentary film maker, and internationally recognized consultant.

Fascinating to me are the compromises that they choose to make to pursue success in their careers—compromises between family and job, between ideals and material gain, between what they would choose to be doing with their lives and the choices they currently make. Our successful corporate executive officer describes her dilemma at its deepest level when she asks: *What am I doing there? Am I endangering my immortal soul? Or am I studying with my Zen Master? Is this all grist for the mill that's going to help me evolve and become united with the One, manifesting One? Or am I squandering and destroying the blessings that I've been given?*

Most of us grapple with our alternative choices and do our best. Few of us get to do it entirely our way. But what stands out is that each of our highly effective people is choosing with eyes wide open, which may well be a most important requirement for becoming an effective person. What we can learn from them are four distinctive, in-depth understandings of how their own assumptions—and those that prevail in the environments in which they apply their professional skills—shape their careers and their personal lives.

Dennis Reynolds

For more than 20 years, Dennis Reynolds has devoted his professional life to the service of young children and their parents. Dennis is Director of the University of Oregon Child Care and Development Centers in Eugene, Oregon, and past member of the Oregon State Commission for Child Care. He is also the father of three children: Ian, now in his 20s; a daughter, Lindsey, a high-school senior; and Nick, a fifth grader. Dennis also survived—or graduated from, depending on how one might look at it—three earlier marriages before he and Suzanne, his current wife, found each other. What is unusual about Dennis as a father is that each of his three children arrived in different prior marriages and he has always actively co-parented all of them, thanks to shared custody arrangements with cooperating ex-spouses.

Deborah Loschiavo

At the time of writing, Deborah Loschiavo is coordinator of the nation's largest Direct Instruction remedial-reading program, currently being implemented in Ft. Worth, Texas. She also counsels to school districts in Michigan and Maryland, implementing similar programs for inner-city schools in Detroit and Baltimore. Deborah holds a master's degree in special education from the University of Oregon. She served for many years in Oregon schools teaching developmentally disabled children, before moving to Texas in 1998, where she accepted an invitation to design and implement the Ft. Worth program.

Deborah lives in Round Rock, Texas, with her husband Bob and their teenage children, Joan and Eliseo. Deborah is the daughter of Joan Spencer (Nikki) Bogart and is, as a consequence, my stepdaughter.

Beth Cameron
(a pseudonym)

"Beth Cameron" is a pseudonym for a highly successful executive officer of a major high-tech company, where she is in charge of the corporation's supplier diversity programs. She explains why she chooses to remain anonymous:

I chose to use a pseudonym for this interview because I believe that my candid discussion of corporate culture might negatively affect my career opportunities in corporations. My experience tells me that any employee or job candidate who is perceived as critical of or not fully embracing the corporation will be rejected or sidelined. Candid observations of problems or deficiencies are perceived as disloyal or traitorous and the hallmark of a troublemaker.

Bruce Milletto

Bruce Milletto is president of Bellissimo, Inc. His early involvement and insights into the American gourmet coffee movement have been written about in numerous national and international trade publications, where he has been hailed as a pioneer of the American espresso industry.

Bruce holds an undergraduate degree from Northern Arizona University and a master's degree from the University of Oregon. He has worked for various corporations and government agencies in marketing and teaching positions, and has also created and owned multiple retail businesses, including three successful gourmet coffee operations. As a consultant, he has assisted numerous clients in creating new coffee start-ups worldwide.

Bruce won the 1999 Distinguished Author Award presented by the Specialty Coffee Association of America and is a frequent contributor to such trade publications as *Fresh Cup Magazine, Fancy Food Magazine, Coffee Culture Magazine* (Canada), and *Speciale Caffé* (Italy). He and his wife, Jan, live in Eugene, Oregon. They have two teenage children, Mathew and Whitney.

9

Assumptions About Parenting

Conversations with Deborah Loschiavo

and Dennis Reynolds

Topic Index

9

Assumptions About Parenting

Conversations with Deborah Loschiavo

and Dennis Reynolds

Parenthood remains the greatest single preserve of the amateur.
—Alvin Toffler

Every beetle is a gazelle in the eyes of its mother.
—Moorish proverb

Don't limit a child to your own learning, for he was born in another time.
—Rabbinical saying

What we do and fail to do as parents impacts future generations in ways we do not fully understand. But we do know that the consequences of our parenting—both good and bad—are long-term and outlast our own lives. How our children will deal with their adulthood and their children is affected by the way we parent them. And each of us has only to look within our own experience and within our own families to know that every one of us still has much to learn about being good parents.

Mastering the art of parenting is a gradual process that starts with the knowledge each of us brings with us when we enter parenthood. We proceed from there with a good deal of trial-and-error experimenting with the lives of our children. Our own assumptions underlie both the knowledge base with which we enter the world of parenting and our subsequent parenting experiences. The parenting scenario becomes even more confused in families where assumptions about parenting are in conflict. And where assumptive confusion reigns, parents and children are apt to swirl about in rudderless boats on stormy seas, often with disastrous consequences.

To help us find our way through the sea of parental confusion to more solid ground, I have called upon two respected professionals in the fields of parenting and childhood education: Dennis Reynolds and Deborah Loschiavo. In this chapter and the next, these two experts share their thinking on the general theme of assumptions about parenting.

Being Like or Unlike One's Parents

Vic: My own experience in working with people is that each of us chooses whether and in what ways we are going to be like or unlike our own parents. Do either of you care to comment?

Dennis: The concerns I have are when people settle for one extreme or the other. They end up either being exactly like their parents, or they're damned if they're going to be anything like their parents. For example, I'm thinking of two nephews of mine whose mom lived a very alternative lifestyle. One nephew is now a born-again Christian, and the other is a born-again Capitalist. He is religiously committed to the pursuit of money.

I remember having a discussion with one of them about, *When was he going to stop rebelling against his parents?* And his response was, *About the same time you stopped rebelling against yours.* That was very perceptive of him. Mine was counterculture rebellion against more conservative parents; his was a conservative rebellion against liberal parents. Ideally, we get to the point where we make our own decisions.

Vic: So, Dennis, you're describing instances of children—in this case both you and your nephews—choosing to be unlike their parents. Deborah, what has been your experience?

Deborah: I have never wanted to *not* be like my mother. I've parented a lot like my mother with regard to the love and affection and ongoing unconditional manner in which she treats me as well as my brothers and sisters. She was a model for that. And also with regard to values. We were raised very much by my grandfather, who had a profound influence on her, so when she wasn't around, she was still the main player. He filtered through her, and you could see the similarity of the two. And I really have used much of what she taught me.

Mother softened my grandfather. He was of a generation where life was much harder, so he was harder. She was softer and transferred those values to me in a way that was much less brutal than he was taught, namely, *You do what's right,* whether or not it *feels* right. In fact, *the way it feels* is one of the last things that you consider. Feelings are not usually reasons for doing things. This is a core value—a core assumption—that's affecting me right now: *You do what needs to be done, and you do it with the greatest amount of character and integrity.* And, *You deal with your feelings privately.* That comes directly from my mother, and that comes directly from her father.

Vic: You have strong models for parenting in your grandfather and mother.

Deborah: Yes, it was clear what their roles were with me.

Mother and I have grown up together. We've known each other now for 47 years. The roles have changed, of course. And I can't remember at what point I stopped being a child with her. I still am, in many ways. She takes care of me, which is wonderful. But we counsel one another. And that has been a wonderful model for me to use with my daughter, Joanie. And I do. I ask Joanie's advice and I listen to it. Her perspective and her perceptions of me in my world are helpful, because she, too, knows me very, very well.

Of course, my daughter is struggling with getting away from me, which is what she needs to be doing. And it's okay with me. Because I know, having gone through it with my mother, that it's not going to be devastating. I know that we're inextricably bound to one another and geography and distance are relative. My mother and my grandmother were geographically close for many years but light years apart.

Vic: So both you and your daughter—well, it's hard to know about your daughter yet—but certainly, you have chosen consciously to be very much like your mother and, in certain ways, like your grandfather.

Deborah: Yes.

Vic: Are there parental figures in your personal life whose values you have chosen to be unlike, whose parenting style you have pushed yourself away from?

Deborah: Well, a piece of parenting that I think was characteristic of the fifties was physical: hitting kids. I consciously decided when my children were born that I wouldn't hit them. I felt that to use physical punishment well, it had to be done judiciously and unemotionally, and I had no models for that. I knew I had a vicious temper, and I knew that I would abuse my children. Danette [Deborah's younger sister] and I have talked about that because we were both hit kids. As a kid who's been hit, not only do you experience being hit but you experience the hitter; and, in our case, the hitter was clearly enraged. So when rage struck me as a young parent, there was an inclination to start swinging. And I decided before I was a parent and pregnant with Joan, that I would not be that way with my kids.

Vic: The hitter was a male?

Deborah: The hitter was my mother. My mother was a hitter. And my father was a hitter. They both were hitters.

Vic: So the same parents you're holding up as positive role models also had parenting traits you've consciously rejected. *I want this, but I don't want that.* You've been selective.

Deborah: Parenting has been a conscious effort with me from the get-go. I figured out, somehow—dumb luck, probably—that some things worked with me and some things didn't work. So when something didn't work, I changed it.

Vic: I'm seeing the difference between unconscious and conscious parenting as basically a difference between knee-jerk reaction to situations and considered choice.

Deborah: Yes, I think that's a usable definition.

You know, as a young child, I saw a lot of impulsive rage from Tony [a stepfather]. He clearly would not have thought about the implications of his behavior for the child he was angry at. For him it was simply a venting, a clearing away of stuff as fast as he could, like sweeping his arm over a table to clear away the dishes. It had nothing to do with the child; it was strictly an outpouring of self-centered rage. I experienced that as a child.

And as an adult, I see people parenting in seemingly thoughtless ways and, of course, everything bad happens. An unconscious life is a life that isn't well lived, and what tends to happen is unpredictable. For the person who's not being thoughtful, I'm sure things seem to come out of nowhere at them.

But I think that all parents are on a continuum of self-awareness. Some people would look at my parenting and say: *She's totally unconscious.* And I look at some people's parenting and say the same thing. The truth is that we are all struggling with the hardest job we will ever have. And making the assumption that someone else is guilty of unconscious parenting is a waste of time. It's judgmental. It's negative. It isn't helpful to anybody. But if you model conscious parenting, you can provide help indirectly because it may lead to someone asking, *How come you do what you do?* Then there's an opportunity

for the conscious parent to teach and for the unconscious parent to learn.

Dennis: I think that those of us who worked with children and
families before we had children of our own may have had an
opportunity to practice being more conscious of how we interact with kids. We've had experience with other people's children that I know I bring to my interaction with my own kids.

Parenting Is (is not) Easy

Vic: On *Oprah* the other day, I saw three 12- and 13-year-old
mothers who said they opted to have babies—purposefully
got pregnant to please their boyfriends—and they said they
thought being a parent was really going to be easy.

Dennis: That is one of the assumptions many people bring to
parenting that is potentially harmful—assumptions such as:
*Parenting is easy. Anybody can do it. You really don't need to spend
that much time doing it.*

Of course, I would not expect a 12- or 13-year-old to have
the sophistication to realize—

Vic: They were a lot more sophisticated a year later.

Dennis: The assumption that *It's easy,* that *It's like falling off a log,*
is so wrong. As is the assumption that *We don't need support in
the process of doing it; we can do it ourselves because people always
have.* Well, people always haven't; they've had the family network. And the assumption that *It doesn't take much time* is a
myth that was perpetrated on the parents of America in the
early eighties with the notion of *Quality Time. Give five minutes a day of quality time.* I think that's a crock. I think it takes
Being there. Yes, quality is important, but so is quantity.

I'm reminded of the Peace Corps slogan that was used for
years: *This is the hardest work you'll ever love.* That's a good sum-
mary of parenting.

I remember taking childbirth classes with one of my partners, and a woman was saying: *We're taking all these classes and*

we're studying pregnancy and neonatal development and what's going on in utero with this baby, but I'm going to have to take this damn thing home, and I don't have a clue about what I'm gonna do with it. I want an owner's manual!

She was asking for just the basics. How do you pin a cloth diaper? It's as if people needed disposable diapers with tape on them because nobody knew how to fold cloth diapers anymore. We have a culture that has lost the basic skill of how to work a safety pin because nobody has time to spend with babies.

My advice to people who want to have a baby: *Go rent first. Go hang out with some babies, and figure some stuff out before you use your first child as a guinea pig.*

Conflict and Polarization

Vic: I stated at the beginning of this chapter that *[t]he parenting scenario becomes even more confused in families where assumptions about parenting are in conflict.* Deborah, can you comment on that?

Deborah: There's a tendency to look at your partner's behavior and react to it. Typically, the woman will take the role of trying to soften what appears to her to be a harsh parenting style in the man. I see this in a lot of my women friends and their husbands. The dads are perceived by the moms as too harsh or disconnected. And in either case the moms compensate.

The inclination for me as the mother is to compensate, and I rationalize that with the fact that my children are extensions of my body. If you've never carried a child and delivered it, you can't know. It is a completely amazing experience to produce a human being.

Vic: And all of a sudden there you are, a mother with all these brand-new feelings and your world is changing—

Deborah: —and you've made another human being. Oh my God! It's just boggling. So anybody . . . *anybody* . . . who hurts that

little person creates in the mother a desire to protect. At least.
And most likely to destroy. [Both burst into laughter]. The
idea is to make sure that doesn't happen again.

Vic: Yeh. You can always find another male lion out there.

Deborah: Oh sure. And that baby triggers the biological propen-
sity for making the species continue. Thank God we do it.

Vic: Where would we be if—

Deborah: —we would be dead. So there really is that desire to be
protective, as long as your child is alive or you're alive.

You saw it this morning with Mother. She just hollered at
you because she didn't want me to have this old coffee. Big
deal! I mean, like I care? But you're under fire immediately.
That happens from the instant the baby is born and cries and
doesn't get picked up fast enough, to when you're almost fifty
years old and your mother doesn't want you to have cold coffee or whatever.

If you really love your partner and really want a happy
marriage and you have children in the home that you've had
together—imagine what it's like if one of you is a steppar-
ent!—what you must do is carefully examine your behavior
with regard to your partner's relationship to the children.

Dennis: As I sit and listen to the two of you, and as a man who has
spent years as a teacher and caregiver of young children, I get
a tad defensive with the implication that mothers are more
nurturing and dads are indifferent "male lions."

Setting Limits

Dennis: People assume that kids respect and are drawn to people
who give in to them. That's not true. When I was a classroom
teacher, I would ask my staff of student aides, *Who is the most
rigid about rules and expectations regarding the kids' behavior in
this place?*

And their response was, *Dennis, you are.*

And who do you think they love and respect the most?

And they said, *They're all gaga over you.*

And I'd ask, *Do you think that maybe there's a connection?*

I went to a classroom today, and one little boy came running over, shouting my name and grabbing my legs. It was a three-year-old who was sent to my office yesterday because he was being bad. I just sat down with him and talked with him about his problems and the fact that his behavior was unacceptable. Then I turned my back on him and went about my business for a while. He loves me! He thinks I walk on water.

I think some parents assume that children are like adults, that they think and respond like little adults. They don't understand that child brains function more like dog brains. They do! Kids' brain size is smaller. They have a wider array of synaptic connections early on than dogs, but they don't know how to sort and make decisions about which ones to use in a particular circumstance.

There's a developmental process that has to happen with kids. I mean, two- and three-year-olds are as egocentric as all hell! They're selfish. And to expect them to be otherwise just leads to problems.

Don't you understand that when you hit your sister with a truck it hurts?

No.

And they really don't. And if they did understand, they wouldn't care. It's not because they're evil; it's because they haven't figured it out yet. Empathy is based on the development of the ability to see another's point of view.

Deborah: I agree. You have to set limits. It's the parent's responsibility to set limits. In the very early stages of children's lives, the limits are salient and the parent dictates them. As the child matures, limits become a point of negotiation and an opportunity to teach negotiation to children.

I really don't care if my children argue with me about limits. I think it's a good skill that they need to develop, because limits are not always right, and you want kids to evaluate them critically. One of the nice things about a dialogue about limits is that it forces the parent to be conscious. And as the dialogue ensues, you begin to compromise, and the compromising teaches the children about their own limits and the parent's as well. It's a dynamic dance. In the beginning, the steps are dictated by the parent; at the end, the steps are mutually agreed upon.

Children are the best! They make you do things that you normally wouldn't want to do, but they make you better people.

Dennis: I agree. Challenging and questioning the limits is a learning process for kids, and letting go of a need to be in control is a learning process for parents.

The Roles Fathers Play

Dennis: I think that as a culture we devalue the role of fathers.

Research shows that kids who have no significant male role model are at higher risk of violent behavior as young men than kids who have good male role models. Fatherless daughters also have higher rates of teen pregnancy.

The most readily available male role models tend to be fathers. And fathers have an incredible impact on young girls who, without a good male role model, have difficulty in establishing adult relationships with men. We learn how to hang out with the other gender by hanging out with that gender. Women learn how to hang out with men by hanging out with men, and usually that means the opportunity to hang out with their fathers.

Deborah: Absolutely right. And the perspective of a strong male role model is critical to the development of young boys. It is a shark-infested ocean out there for little boys, and the rules that govern how men are in society are very different from those that govern women. Who better to teach them to a boy than a loving father? There's no way they are too young to not benefit from that. The converse is that the father benefits tremendously from contact with the child.

Dennis: We still think in terms of moms staying home with the kids. There's an assumption that *care of children is women's work,* and that *women are inherently better at it.* Some women are, some women aren't. There are different types of personalities, male and female, and some are more nurturing and responsive than others.

In my ideal world there would be a parenting curriculum starting in elementary school for both sexes, where they would bring in babies, and boys and girls would play with and care for them.

Vic: Is this being done anywhere?

Dennis: It's being done on an experimental basis, but when the grant runs out, it stops.

Vic: And that's the end of it?

Dennis: I haven't seen anything that's been replicated on a continuing basis. I think I ended up working in child care because my sister moved back in with her kid when I was thirteen, and she handed me this infant and said, *Here, I'm going out and you need to babysit.* And I had to figure out how to deal with an infant when I was 13 years old. So when I was 27 years old and I had an infant who was my son, I already had had some time to figure out how to deal with it.

In an isolated nuclear family in America, we sometimes see a mother and father with the first baby they've ever come across now living with them—twenty-four hours a day. It's a formula for disaster.

Vic: What do you say about that to women who are single moms?

Deborah: To the involuntary single mother I say, Good luck! Keep at it and gird your loins, baby, because you're doing an impossible job.

To the self-selected single woman parent, I struggle with what to say because it is a two-sex society, and I feel a need for little girls and boys to know the male perspective. They will be raised in a world that is male and female and is largely a male power structure within which they'll need to function—successfully. You can't fight it, because you will be consumed and destroyed by it if you do. You have to conform. It's a changeable world. It's malleable, certainly, but only if you know how to play the game. Only if you know the rules. And who better to teach it than a male.

I think that the involuntarily single mom—the woman who was divorced, abandoned, never given a shot at a real relationship for whatever reason—is not playing with a full deck. She has to do it all. And I would hate to do it all as a woman. I don't think she can do it all in terms of providing a male perspective and male support.

Children need fathers. I truly believe that. I didn't for years; now I do. I truly believe there is male energy, and it is good for children. It is wonderful for children. I think male energy is about nurturing, it's about strength, it's about doin' hard stuff, it's about gettin' the job done. At its best, it is direct, it is warm, it is honest, it is enduring; and to deprive a child of access to that is not okay. If one is in an abusive situation, you need to get them out of it. But to choose to not have a man in a child's life is a poor choice. I don't think it's right.

That child of yours needs a dad. She needs somebody who tosses her around, grabs her by the hands and drags her up and down the street with him, and tells jokes that Mom would never find funny. Male energy is very different from female energy, and it plays a role in the development of a child who will have to function in a society of men and women.

Typically, young girls raised without men have very difficult times having relationships with men as young women. But in the lives of children there may be men who are not their fathers who can model that stuff, who can have that energy and provide those experiences for the children that may suffice. I've known children who were raised in extremely abusive situations but were given little doses of healthy situations and thrived and turned into healthy adults.

Vic: So the single mom might find safe male models for her kid.

Deborah: Absolutely. And be real smart about not terrifying them. Teachers, uncles, brothers, all of those men can suffice. But they need to be enduring in their commitment to that child because we don't want to pass on the rule that they're nice, but they're temporary and unreliable.

Balancing Economic and Parenting Needs

Vic: Dennis, picking up on your earlier comments about the importance of *being there* as a parent for your child, how do you deal with the demands of the economy for both parents to be in full-time jobs? For example, I saw a recent article in *The New York Times* on exactly this subject. An X-generation couple were saying that they had to make radical adjustments to balance the demand for both parents to be working and at the same time not giving up on parenthood. Their dilemma, *How are we going to do this?* was particularly challenging. Can you talk about that?

Dennis: I can give you specifics. I administer child-care programs. Our assistant director spent the summer working four days a week so she could spend more time with her kids and so her three-year-old wouldn't have to spend as much time in child care.

Those of us who work in child care know that it's not the optimum situation for kids to spend hours and hours in child care every day. A lot of the answer is to look for balances: Work at home for a portion of time. Swap time for some days off. I worked a nine-tenths contract for several years so I could have one day off with my son every other week when he was still in preschool. And that was really enough time to be close. So it's making adjustments.

Working a point-nine made a real difference in the amount

of time I had with my kids, particularly when they weren't with me full-time. Lindsey once observed that she spent more time with me—living with me a third of the time—than she did with her mother because they just didn't spend as much time together. She was at her mother's house more, but her mother wasn't home.

One of the most important pieces of federal legislation that we passed in this country was the Parental Leave Law. People can have 12 weeks. I spent three months at home with Lindsey when she was six months old, and we made a connection that is there forever. I had a similar opportunity with Nick.

Deborah: Balancing economic and parenting needs is such a timely topic for me, because right now that's exactly what I'm doing.

Clearly, economic needs have to be met before you can do anything else. You need to have a place to live and food to eat. Ideally, you live with someone who does that—or does it as well as you do, or does it along with you.

It's a dynamic balancing act. It changes with the ages of the children and the economic situation in your life.

Ideally, one would have enough money to parent at will, as it were. I would hate to be trapped at home, and I would hate to be trapped away from home. The emotional and intellectual needs of children are at least as important as the money. Of course, if you don't have money, you can lose your family. But short of that, you must always balance. You have to be constantly looking at the developmental stage of your children and provide them with as much emotional security and support as they need.

And I agree with Dennis regarding "quality time." There ain't no such thing. The truth is, your kids need all of your time. They need as much parenting time as you can give them. Quality time is stupid. What makes a life for a child is mundane, is routine, is constant. It's not coming in with 24-carat experiences for that child to treasure while they're with some generic caretaker. Where your hearts are formed are in tying shoes and running baths and clearing tables and talking about school days, knowing so intimately the details of your child's life that you can ask specific questions and be responsive to their little snippets of information that they give you without the questions.

So it's a balancing act in time.

Depending upon your economic situation, the balancing act can demand excruciating, difficult decisions. The difficult decision is to abandon your dreams of a career for the sake of the child because—I truly believe this—the child needs to be the priority in the early years especially. And that was something I didn't learn until the early years were gone.

As the relationship grows, the child becomes a source of comfort and love for the parent. Being forced away from the children by economic needs is hard on all members of the family.

Many of us are blessed with careers and full rich lives, so the balancing act becomes a kind of a nagging bitchy problem that we whine about to our girl friends over our gelatos. But for a majority of parents, it is the harsh reality of leaving our children with strangers, to work at jobs that bring in enough money for another month of bills, to be repeated ad infinitum. The children are raised by other people who tie their shoes and listen to their days. And that's a terrible sadness. That's a loss for everyone. It's a loss in the transfer of values to our children and in modeling parenting. You need to be there for your kid's first word. It really solidifies that experience of being a parent. And yet at the same time you have to be able to pay for the rent and pay for food.

Those are the realities for a lot of people.

The Need for a Moral Compass

Dennis: In our country there's a widespread view that we have lost the sense of a moral compass. I'm reading more about how we've neglected the spiritual side and we're not giving our kids an awareness that there's more out there than just immediate day-to-day gratification.

The optimist in me thinks we are responding to that. At the one extreme, people are home-schooling their kids because schools are sinful, and at the other extreme we've got folks who are sending their kids to Waldorf schools. But all those folks aren't so far apart. It's almost as if they've come around a circle, one going right and one going left and coming to similar points that recognize *a spiritual essence is missing here.*

As a society and culture we've become increasingly secular. I think that has cost us. It comes at the expense of kids who are expected to find their own sense of right and wrong.

Deborah: Teenagers are interesting to me because they push you to where you have to ask yourself serious and fundamental questions about why you do what you do and why you require them to do what you require them to do.

I suppose if you are religious, you can avoid such questions by laying the blame on God! I've not been religious for most of my life, so that hasn't been an option for me, but as I age, I am becoming increasingly religious, or spiritually aware. In fact, I've not been secular for the last fifteen years. But I've been defining more and more clearly what I mean by that. And I've been talking to my children about my core values regarding why we're here and what our task is.

My core value is that we're here to love each other and the task is to serve each other. And from that springs the value of Right Behavior. I use those as the points on the moral compass. Right Behavior becomes more accessible. We don't talk about what *feels* right, only that you *know* what's right. It may not be fun, but you *know* what the right action is here, in this situation.

I talk with the children a lot. As they mature, their behavior has consequences that are much greater and much more serious than it was even five years ago. And because they are young, emerging beings, I want them to be conscious humans. And I want them to understand the basis from which they make their decisions. So I believe we need a moral compass, and I believe that I'm giving them one.

As we get older as parents, *Because I said so!* no longer carries the weight it did. It works with little children because they truly believe you are God. But when you become fallible to them—at the point at which they reach some Piagetian stage where they can look at you and see a human being and not a God—you need to call forth something bigger.

So, I think for me, my children have created—in fact, this brings me to a whole other area that you haven't addressed here that may be of interest to you.

Vic: Go ahead and address it.

Our Children Are Our Teachers

Deborah: This other area that I mentioned has to do with the positive impact children can have on their parents in terms of giving them a reason to become good people and become conscious, thoughtful people. Because you love these little things so much, you can't just live in some arbitrary way; you have to start examining your life. Then you become models for them, and that carries a huge load. You know you can't get drunk and stoned and stupid because you don't want them to; because you know it's really awful and hurts a lot. So they become the moral compass for the parent in many ways.

Doing what will further their reach for divinity becomes a reason for cleaning up your act. They ask very hard questions, and you need to do very serious work on yourself to give answers you're willing to let them live with. You become their model, and that calls for tremendous amounts of self-examination and lint-picking of one's navel.

But often it's the other way around: it's the children who provide the moral compass. They truly do. Just recently, I have found in my children a reason to not become totally self-destructive in what has been an extremely traumatic experience for me. I cannot go to pieces because they need me to be solid. I can't afford to be crazy.

I have to do my very best because they need a mom. And they need a mom who under adversity does the right thing. That's where they come in as the moral compass. Unknowingly to them.

It's a dialogue, a moral dialogue I have with my children in terms of my own behavior. They watch me. They've seen me fall apart. They've seen me pick myself back up, dry my tears, put on my professional outfit, get my presentation, stand up in front of those people, do a bang-up job, and make my money. They've seen me do the right thing.

Being a parent is the best thing I've ever done in my life. I love that part of my life. So they actually form the moral compass, and I form the moral compass. We're almost in tandem.

Vic: Among all of you a moral compass emerges.

Deborah: And the whole issue of the need for a moral compass, I think, is an inevitable outcome of conscious living.

I think the main thing about parenting—an assumption made by young parents—is that they are the teachers of their children. And that assumption is changed. If they pay attention, they realize they are the student as much as the teacher. The gifts flow both ways. The lessons flow both ways. You must let go of the assumption that you have to know it all and be all. You're in this together. There's a 20- or 30- or 40-year difference in age, but you're all progressing along on your own journeys, and you have things to give each other.

Vic: You have been making the point that parenting really needs to be conscious behavior on the part of parents. The assumption that you don't have to think about it, don't have to work at it, don't have to consider how to be a parent, is erroneous.

Deborah: I think it is beyond erroneous. I think it's tragic. I think an unexamined life . . . why bother? And a person who doesn't examine being a parent misses so much opportunity for personal growth. That is the gift in it.

Dennis: I see it as a two-for-one opportunity for growth. The individual who strives to be a conscious, open parent creates an opportunity for his or her personal growth and also models conscious living for the children. When and if that generation parents, they may do it even better than we did.

It is, in reality, one part of a continuing evolution of the human species. It's the gift that keeps on giving.

WHAT TO DO ABOUT THEM

I. Respond to the following:

1. List five assumptions that guide you in your parenting role.
2. How did you come by each of these assumptions? Are they similar to or different from those of your own parents?
3. Can you identify the role models you use to shape your own parenting style?
4. How well are your assumptions about parenting working? Are you satisfied or dissatisfied with your parenting and its results?
5. How clearly do you and your partner communicate with each other about your parenting? What happens when conflict between you surfaces over parenting issues? Can you identify some of the conflicting assumptions involved?

II. Which of the following assumptions about parenting do you share?

· *My child can't seem to do anything right without my direction.* [Share/Don't share]
· *Parenting is easy, and you really don't need to spend that much time doing it.* [Share/Don't share]
· *The most important time for parents to be there for the child is in infancy.* [Share/Don't share]
· *Women are inherently better at child care than men.* [Share/Don't share]
· *Kids respect and are drawn to people who give in to them.* [Share/Don't share]
· *Children are like adults in that they think and respond like little adults.* [Share/Don't share]

Notes & Comments

Notes & Comments

Notes & Comments

10

Parenting Children
with Special Needs

Conversations with Deborah Loschiavo

and Dennis Reynolds

Topic Index

10

Parenting Children with Special Needs

Conversations with Deborah Loschiavo

and Dennis Reynolds

Of course, all children have special needs, so the chapter title is somewhat ambiguous. I thought of *exceptional children* as an alternative, but the same ambiguity applies: Every child is unique and therefore exceptional. Regardless of title, in this chapter we examine the special problems of parenting those children who have been deprived of the prerequisites for their healthy growth and development.

As in all chapters, our particular interest is to seek out and identify the underlying assumptions of parents and others that result in the situations they face.

Again in this chapter, the views expressed are those of our two experts in childhood early development and remedial education, Dennis Reynolds and Deborah Loschiavo.

Parenting Special-Needs Children

Deborah: As a special-ed preschool teacher, I spent years talking with parents and knowing parents and caring a lot for parents. Certain samenesses began to emerge in their way of being the parents of young, developmentally delayed children. Those people taught me a lot about being a parent and about the different requirements of parenting a child who is clearly deviant.

This subclass of parents is unique. There are basic parenting skills that must be in place for all parents to function effectively, and then there's a different layer for the parents of developmentally delayed children. Those people have to be extraordinary to raise these children. That's an assumption that I make, having watched them struggle with tiny babies, preschoolers, elementary-age children, and on up through adulthood. I've known parents of developmentally delayed individuals from birth to probably 25 or 30 or older. They are different from parents of normally developing children.

They are different because they are largely unsupported by the community. Most of us have moms and dads who had normal children, so they are parents of normal children. If I were a parent of a developmentally delayed child, my ability to identify with my parents' parenting would end at some point. To raise this child, I'd have to do extraordinary things that I have no model for. And I would discover that my community could support me only to the extent that I could find in it other parents of children with developmental delays. Finding other members of that class of parents is critical for their survival and for the survival of their marriages and their families. It is an intensely negative and destructive potential force to have a child with a developmental disability.

Vic: Sounds terribly discouraging.

Deborah: It is discouraging if the parents are unsupported. I taught probably 150 preschool children directly and knew their parents. And I knew probably 100 middle-school parents. Of that sample of 250 parents of developmentally delayed people—children and adults—there were some avatars. People who were joyful and funny and happy and well and engaged with their lives and in love with their partners—people who clearly had figured it out.

Vic: How do you define "avatar"?

Deborah: I have my own special definition: A person who is able to take the lead, who inspires. A person who blazes the trail.

These are the people who form the communities, the people who demand changes in the system. These are the parents who keep at home their profoundly retarded autistic son who's incredibly destructive, and they live with that child in a way that doesn't destroy their marriage and their lives.

People I call avatars do regular things in regular ways with very difficult children that other people, myself included, are not able to do. These are inspirational people. And usually their children don't grow out of their afflictions, they don't change. Many times they get worse, but some of them get better with the cooperation of parents and teachers and a wonderful support group.

The avatars are those parents who become stronger. They become leaders, they become legislators. They are the people who change the laws for services to the handicapped. They are the ones who make those things happen because people of normal children don't understand.

Another assumption I make is that professionals who are themselves parents are better able to deal with the parents of their students, be they normal or not. When I was a young professional before I was married, I thought that was a bunch of hooey, that there was nothing a parent could know that I didn't already know. That is an incorrect assumption.

Vic: It helps to have been there.

Deborah: It sure does. Being a parent has made it a lot easier. The parents of the kids will come to me and say, "I don't know what to do? I'm not sleeping nights," or "She's not eating" or whatever, and I can truthfully say, "I know how you feel." And we can connect at that level, and then I can pull out my bag of tricks and say, "Here are some things that work for some

people." Connecting at that level was so critical to their being
receptive to my ideas.

Dennis: There is also another dynamic involved here. When parents have confidence both in our professional expertise and
our own experience as parents, their receptiveness to professional intervention is increased.

Being There for Bonding Time

Vic: Another assumption that is widely accepted is that all children have a special need to bond with their moms, in particular, but also with their dads.

Dennis: Bonding happens very early. I have some very strong bi-
ases about bonding time being the most important time in
terms of shaping the structure of the brain. More and more
research shows that simply touching babies and being with
babies increases their cognitive ability. Unfortunately, group
child care, which can be done very well, still ends up with 4:1
and 3:1 ratios, and babies don't get touched as much as they
do in a home-based setting. Or can. Lots of parents park the
kid in front of the TV, and that doesn't help.

The American Academy of Pediatrics has urged that children under two not watch television at all. They need human
contact—touching, caressing and real conversation.

The assumption that *parenting counts more when a kid gets
a little older and can talk to you* is incorrect. It really counts
much more at the very beginning. The more I read, the more
I observe, the more certain I am that *the most important time for
parents to be there is in infancy.* That first year.

So it is about balances and trade-offs. I see far too many
kids who spend too much time in child care because parents
feel, *We need to make more money.* But sometimes they're needing to make more money just to pay the incredibly expensive
child-care bill. But if the child doesn't have good experiences
as an infant, it's not going to be successful in the finest educa-

tion systems available; the linkages, the synapses in the brain will not have been formed because those happen early.

Deborah: You know, I would almost say as a parent, though the child-development experts may not agree, that bonding time lasts a lifetime. I mean, in the very beginning there truly is a biological time for connection, when you first deliver a baby. And I think it's pretty clear now about how long it takes and how much time a parent needs with his or her infant for that to occur.

But I would argue that bonding continues throughout the life of the parent, assuming the parent dies first. Because the child, especially during the first twenty years of his or her life and maybe after that—I don't have the experience of parenting anybody over twenty—evolves into different people and you have to connect with each different person. The so-called essential-core person is forming over those years. That core person doesn't really exist, it's an amorphous thing, and as the child evolves into a new form, you bond with that new child.

Vic: It occurs to me that there are also the changes in the parent.

Deborah: Then there's that. Yeh, that's exactly right.

Vic: So you have a "new parent" and a "new child," always evolving their relationship, transforming and changing it as they themselves transform and change, and as their needs for each other change. Makes sense?

Deborah: Makes perfect sense. I've always characterized it as sort of a hallucination. I mean, you just watch it unfold, and the watcher is unfolding along with the watched.

Vic: The watchee?

Deborah: The watchee. It goes back to: *The observer dictates reality.* There's nothing static. The parent doesn't stay the same at all. And that's a wonderful thing. And if you can establish the communication, the parent learns from the child and the child from the parent. A rich source of personal information develops because they know each other so well.

Bonding takes *time*. It goes back to *time*. You have to spend time together—not take them to that fabulous movie or buy them that incredible whatever they've been dying for. Uh-uh. They'll never remember that. They will remember *the time*. That's what it's about.

Dennis: And it doesn't really matter how you spend that time. Sometimes digging a ditch in the backyard together is as memorable as an expensive vacation. The important factor is that the time is spent together

Child Care's Track Record

Vic: Dennis, you mentioned before that placing a child in a child-care situation may not be an adequate response to the child's needs. Can you say more about that?

Dennis: The industry that I'm a part of does not have a good track record. Research indicates that upwards of 60 percent of child care in America is mediocre to poor. Most of it is not very good. But parents don't even want to look at that. They assume that their kid is in a good situation because to accept the opposite is just so devastating to any parent who cares about the child. They would wallow in guilt and not be able to get any work done, even if they did go to work.

So the assumptions, *We have a quality child-care system, and the kids will be just fine*, or *They'll catch up when they start to school*, just don't hold up as true.

We also have an incredible confidence in professionals, whether they are in the school or in child care. *They'll know. The professionals will know what the kid needs.*

Vic: Is it your view that the assumptions about professionals knowing it all or having the answers are faulty assumptions?

Dennis: Yes. We professionals may have knowledge. But in a classroom of 25 kids we don't necessarily have the ability to do what one parent can do with one child. We simply can't touch kids the way parents can.

I worked in an infant program once, and I remember a particular instance when I had a baby in each arm. A toddler fell down in front of me and came up and hung on my knees crying, wanting and legitimately needing to be comforted, and I couldn't help him. It was like: *Sorry, no room at the inn.* This 4:1 ratio only goes so far.

And yes, we talk about how people used to have 10 kids, but they didn't have 10 babies. And the older ones helped take care of the littler ones. There were a lot of people around to help out. And there was contact and connection. There was physical stimulation and massage and cooing and just blabbering at babies.

Today, people are just too busy and are looking for external fixes, but the most important thing to do with babies is just touch them, and the second most important thing is to talk to them. Doesn't matter what you say. Just touch 'em and blabber.

Vic: The feeling that I'm getting from you is that, as a nation, we're in a hell of a mess with regard to parenting.

Dennis: We've made some missteps, and I think they're across cultures and across class levels too. I think we've become more passive as a nation.

My reflection is based on two items of technology: television and cars. We used to carry our children places; now maybe we carry them to the car. We put them in car seats and strollers, isolate them in these conveyance mechanisms rather than carry them around. In indigenous cultures babies are always strapped on, and that's what babies should be. They should have maximum opportunity for human contact. Now, instead of families talking, families watch television. That's not interactive like a parent talking to a child.

Vic: Deborah, what is your opinion of child care's track record?

Deborah: [Emits a Bronx cheer] Horrible! Just horrible! Unregulated, unreliable, uncertified, untrained, underpaid, high turnover, luck of the draw if you get a decent person, luck of the draw if they do a good job with your kid. No amount of money protects you. You gotta do it yourself if you want it done right.

And I can hear those parents with little children exclaiming, *That's easy for you to say! You're not home all the time with the little shits.* The truth is, child care is a nightmare. For people with handicapped children? Multiplied. It's a horrible situation.

We need to pay child-care workers huge amounts of money; we need to train them to death and do ongoing in-service; we need to monitor them constantly. And who should do that? Well, if I were Queen of the World it would be parent committees that did it. And we would teach them about child development, we would teach them how to teach, we would teach them the kinds of things children need in their lives to develop normally, and we would make sure it happened, and we would make sure they're competent, and we would stay on top of it. Because theirs is the most important job.

Vic: Right. In your domain as Queen of the World, where would the money come from?

Deborah: I think we would treat child care as a critical profession, as we treat basketball. You know, the very best teachers of the youngest would be paid the most and provided with accolades and interviews on the *Today* show. They would be treated as extraordinary people. And *they would be extraordinary people* because the standards for child care would be established by people who loved their children most. And they would know what it looks like.

We already know what it doesn't look like, and it doesn't look like a 15:1 ratio of infants to a worker who's overworked, underpaid, undertrained, exhausted and seventeen. And that's the situation now. The working poor have no choices in child care. It's unconscionable because their children are being raised without parents, essentially. And I'm infuriated by it.

Attachment-disordered Behavior

Dennis: I do think that for kids who are profoundly disturbed, a lot of their issues have to do with attachment disorder. The foundation for secure attachments with other human beings in adulthood is established in attachments with primary caregivers during your first year. Unfortunately for kids trapped in a revolving door of caregivers, they don't securely attach to anybody.

Having secure, solid attachments with people who meet your needs for unconditional love in the first year of your life is the key to healthy development for the rest of your life. It can be one significant caregiver or, as in the village concept, there can be multiple significant caregivers. But it requires that if you can't be there, somebody else has to. Or you can form a tag team for being there and get as many people on your team as you can. Check out people who attend your church for a social network. There are people in churches all over who love babies, people like me. Give me somebody with a baby, and I'll do child care one night a week free, gratis.

Deborah: Having been a special-ed teacher, I worked with many children who were diagnosed with attachment-disordered behavior. They're horrible children to try to be close to. It's very, very painful.

These are children who, for whatever reason, were not given an opportunity to bond with their parent. But I think it's more than that. I think it's lack of bonding combined with prolonged, forced detachment of the child through abuse and neglect. And abandonment. And it creates in the child, for reasons I don't understand—and I can only talk from my experience with these children—they simply have a hell of a time creating enduring bonds with anybody else.

That closes the door on everything, on so much in their lives. And for people trying to connect with them—because we know that's what is good for them—it's thankless in many cases. You really have to find your succor and sustenance else-where. Because the child will make ten years of connection and then let it go in a heartbeat. They drop it real fast.

I worked with an Indian child in Madras, Oregon. She was my student for three years. She was the child of alcoholics. She described herself as being drunk every weekend since she was three. She couldn't remember when she wasn't drunk on a weekend. She was extremely volatile. She would walk into the classroom screaming and swearing, and she would start throw-ing desks. She was about five feet tall, probably weighed a hundred pounds, but a ball of fire and fury. It took me years before she would talk to me in a conversation that wasn't mostly pretty incendiary. I knew she could blow any minute. She was extremely and severely an emotionally disordered kid. She had never been loved unconditionally. Never felt loved, never felt important.

But at some point she began to trust me, and we began to have daily talks. I would always make myself be in the office at a certain time, and Dawn would come by. Some days she would simply come in to tell me how somebody fucked her over and she was mad, but she would always come by. And some days she would sit in my office and sob and cry and wail about what a godawful mess her life was, and her mother's life, and her father's life, and drive-by shootings, and people who had died. She was always being abused—sexually and every other way. And social service was involved, but nothing was coming of it, and I mean the child was a god-awful walking-wounded casualty.

I just knew that she needed to have some anchor. And she was not the only one. Many of my Indian students were that way. My office was full of kids every morning. I would get there, they would fill it up. So I stopped taking calls and stopped doing my e-mail because the kids were my priority. They needed to talk to me. They would sit in my chairs, sharpen my pencils, walk away with my pencils, they would touch my things, they would play with my hair, they would just be with me.

And then, in March, I told all of the kids that I'd be leaving at the end of the school year. These were eighth graders who would be going on to ninth grade in high school and would be leaving me anyway. Shortly after I said that, Dawn threw a horrible fit in one of my classes, called me a fucking bitch and left. And never spoke to me again. Ever. She never came by the office. I passed her in the hall and always spoke, and she never spoke to me again. Because I had done it to her.

That is a case study of an attachment-disordered child. She dared to get connected and couldn't understand, although she was leaving for high school and I wouldn't be seeing her anyway. The fact that I was leaving Madras did it for her. It was over. That is characteristic of attachment-disordered kids; they form very tenuous connections, and then they break them very quickly and irrevocably.

And that's a burden for a special-ed teacher. You must know that when you work with those kinds of children, because you can offend them, and it takes a long time to undo that, if it can be done. They perceive abandonment in everything. They are very hard to teach because you can't get that connection with them. They don't trust you. They have no reason to trust you. They've never had an adult be trustworthy. They've only been abandoned, and it's a real sadness to me to know that I reinforced that in Dawn. That's the reality of my life.

Those children need to be parented; they need somebody who will take them for the rest of their lives. I don't know if those people exist. If you commit to taking a detachment-disordered child into your life, you need to be there for that child for the long haul. And that child will leave you, and that's as it should be. But it's hard. It's thankless.

Dennis: I think the saddest part is that attachment disorder is a preventable disease. There is an immunization: providing the love early in life that shows kids what loving is. A healthy start, a positive first phase of life lays the foundation upon which further growth is built. Fixing the problem later is not impossible, but preventing the problem is less costly, both in emotional investments and in costs of services.

Teenage Parents and Their Parenting

Dennis: We are actually beginning to make some progress in the opposite direction from where we were going for a number of years. Teen pregnancies are starting to go down a little bit.

Vic: Is the quality of parenting among teens going up at all?

Dennis: It's hard to know. There are lots of programs out there for teen parents. They do get a lot of support. They need more. Here in Eugene I know of quite a few programs, but there are some big holes. Programs are attempts to fill the holes that used to be filled by family members. Young girls, 15, 16 years old, would get pregnant and they'd have babies, but back then, they would live with their mother and their aunt and their grandmother and their uncles and their cousins, and there'd be a substantial support network that was family-based. It's the isolated nuclear family consisting of one 16-year-old parent and one child that poses an incredibly high-risk situation.

We've seen some good trends in terms of providing a variety of social supports for teenage parents. In Oregon we're trying to recognize the needs of young parents and trying to keep them in school. We now have a Family Leave law; we have tax incentives for companies to provide more family support. We are at least acknowledging some of the issues.

I don't think we've made *great* progress. The welfare-to-work trend really scares me. We don't have an adequate supply of quality alternative situations for kids when assistance says the moms have to be at work. Maybe every fourth one of them could be taking care of the other three kids. That would provide some welfare-to-work for 25 percent of the clients; you could turn them into child-care workers.

Deborah: I don't have a lot of experience with teenagers who are parents, except for my sister and a friend, and in both cases they were terrible parents. They were still children themselves. They still had their own needs as developing human beings. And though biologically able to have children, they didn't have the repertoire, the skills, the perspective. They didn't have any of the infrastructure together to even start storing the stuff. Teenage parents are handicapped dually: they're too young, and they do not have the dad or a partner to help them.

Vic: And becoming a teenage parent really shapes the rest of their lives.

Deborah: Oh yes. They're already, almost without exception, economically disadvantaged. Every single thing that could be wrong with a parenting situation into which to bring a child is there. They are totally unequipped to have the child, have no money to support the child, have no support system to help them have the child. The exceptions are the black children, who often have their mothers and grandmothers and great-grandmothers, who themselves had babies in their early years.

Vic: The multigenerational families.

Deborah: Yes, and the assumption is that the child will have a child young. The new baby isn't going to be born into an ideal situation by any stretch, but the pregnant teenager has a support system in the form of the mothers and, perhaps, fathers in her family, although I'm fairly certain there are not a lot of males in those contexts.

What I do know is that children of teenagers tend to grow up faster than children of older parents because they need to assume more responsibility younger. I think it's a very bad idea. We need to make it stop. It's bad for the babies and it's very bad for the teenagers.

It seems that when the child is born, the parent's development ceases to be the focus for that parent. And that is as it should be, because the focus needs to go off the parent-child and onto the child-child. And that means that the development of the parent-child—the teenager—is truncated and becomes distorted. Growth continues but in weird ways because it's mashed flat by economic deprivation and lack of support and enormous demands and general inadequacy.

The good news is that teenage pregnancy seems to be going down in this country.

But it's a conundrum.

Mentoring as Parenting

Dennis: Another part of the parenting picture is the mentoring that takes place outside of biological parenting or in custodial parenting.

Vic: Talk about that.

Dennis: Well, I'm reminded of the situation that made headlines not too long ago about two babies switched at birth. This woman loves the kid she had for three years, and the fact that she's not the kid's biological parent has nothing to do with it. She loves that child simply because she loves that child. And by loving that child, her love for the child grew, simply because she fed it with love. So there's that side of it. The assumption that *parent-child love is biologically based* is not correct.

I wish the phrase hadn't become so trite, but it takes the whole village to raise a child. And in many cultures that has been a tradition. I have a photo in my office of Chief Plenty Coups, a Crow Indian, and in Native American culture the chief had parental responsibilities for every child. The photo was given to me by one of the teachers, who is Sioux and Mandan, and he was basically saying, *You're the chief around here. You have responsibility for all these children.*

I think that's an appropriate image to have. Our leaders

should have responsibility for all of our children. And the responsibilities include things like funding school budgets and making sure that support systems and regulations are in place to assure the best-quality child care. As a culture and society, when we make decisions like welfare-to-work, we need to look at the impact it will have on children.

The assumption that you can't really affect a child's life if you're not the parent is false. And I think more and more people are realizing that mentoring programs are incredibly rewarding both for the children involved and for the mentors. A woman I know is involved in Committed Partners for Youth, a local mentoring program, and it's energized her. She talks about *my kid*, and if all of us assume more responsibility for more kids as *my kid*, we'll have healthier kids.

Suzanne and I taught a class on sexuality for high-school kids at our church, and it was wonderful. It's like, I have my own kids, but now I feel as if I have more kids that are a little bit *my kids*.

I moved from being a revolutionary to an evolutionary when I started working with kids, and one of my teachers said, *We're going to change the world one child at a time.* She said that, and I'm going, *Yes!* We *can* make a better world one child at a time if each adult would spend some time parenting—nurturing, loving unconditionally, some kid. Their own, if they've got 'em. But there are lots of them available if they don't have biological children.

Vic: Getting back to the single moms, what about mentoring provided by more mature moms to single moms to help the teenagers to learn how to parent? Are you aware of any such program?

Deborah: Yes. In many high-school programs, that's what those programs are about. Providing them with all of the nuts and bolts along with the emotional support. Most of the programs have as a component a support group where they just talk, and the teacher, presumably a mother herself—it would be stupid if she wasn't, so let's assume she's a mother herself—provides the young teenage mother with counseling and mentoring.

But do you know what those young moms need a lot of? It's the nuts and bolts. They need to know how to change diapers, what to do with earaches, what to do with croup, and what to expect in normal child development. And many of them don't have their moms and grandmoms to teach them, so that is a part of those programs. The best programs.

Dennis: There are also a few exceptional programs that include teen fathers in the mix. They support whatever level of involvement these young men can commit to and provide mentorship and support for them.

Men to mentor these young dads and teen moms and be uncles to the babies can help us to recreate the extended family/clan networks we recognized as the best way to bring up babies.

Vic: Thank you both.

WHAT TO DO ABOUT THEM

With which of the following assumptions do you agree? Disagree?

- *Parenting counts more when a kid gets a little older and can talk to you.*
- *An unconscious life is a life that isn't well lived.*
- *There ain't no such thing as "quality time."*
- *We're here to love each other, and the task is to serve each other.*
- *It's the parent's responsibility to set limits. In the very early stages of children's lives, the parent dictates the limits. As the child matures, limits become a point of negotiation and an opportunity to teach negotiation to children.*
- *Parenting needs to be conscious behavior on the part of parents.*
- *A person who doesn't examine being a parent misses much opportunity for personal growth.*
- *Professionals who are themselves parents are better able to deal with the parents of their students.*
- *The most important time for parents to be there with their child is in infancy.*

Notes & Comments

Notes & Comments

11

Making It in the Corporate World

Conversation with Beth Cameron

Topic Index

11

Making It in the Corporate World

Conversation with Beth Cameron

Vic: I want to explore with you the assumptions that have shaped your career in the corporate world. With what assumptions did you enter the world of business? How have they shifted over time? What have been their consequences? What assumptions have been wide of the mark?

Beth: It's interesting. I was just interviewed by two professors from the UC Berkeley Department of Sociology who are doing a study on diversity in corporate culture. One of their questions was: Are corporations practicing true diversity of race, gender and physical ability? They were exploring whether we really do value diversity and whether diversity as practiced makes a difference.

Vic: Whether corporations are just paying lip service, or are they practicing genuine diversity?

Beth: Yes. I said that I don't see corporate America making use of the diversity it has. Instead, its own strong culture demands that all members—no matter their diverse backgrounds, diverse thought processes, diverse genders, diverse ethnicities, diverse ways of thinking—conform to the corporate culture's model for ways of being in the world.

So, to get to your question, one of the assumptions I made coming in—that a lot of women I saw in law school make—was that because so many of us were doing so well and having so much to contribute, we would become a force for cultural change in law firms and corporate law departments. What I found instead was so many women being beaten down by the dominant culture we entered or being co-opted by the dominant culture. I saw many women concede that they could not change the culture and then leave or become part-timers and fringy in the sense of not going in and taking leadership positions, or they would find ways to just survive—go to work to make their salaries but not really put themselves into position to change the culture.

I've lived through a lot of assumptions about corporate culture. One was that the culture would welcome the new perspective women would bring and would change to incorporate that perspective. Another was that I could easily adapt. When I was first in the legal department, I turned to one of my allies, a male attorney whom I always regarded as a duck in water. Everything rolled off him; the more stressful and impossibly demanding our work became, the funnier he got, because he had a great sense of humor.

Vic: Humor is a great coping mechanism.

Beth: Yes, so I stayed close to him and tried to learn. But he wasn't in Zone A either, because he had too much irony and wit to fit into the corporate culture model; he was too irreverent to be seen as a core leader. Back then I said to him, *You know, I would feel more comfortable being in a tribal ceremony drinking blood out of a skull cup than I feel working here.*

I've traveled a lot. I've lived in different cultures and had a lot of different cultural experiences. I thought I was extremely good at adapting to other cultures and shape-shifting and being able to savor other cultures, no matter how different they were from my base culture and my own belief systems. Adapting to the corporate culture has been the most challenging.

But I think that I certainly have adapted. I know the language now. I know what's expected in terms of how I talk and how I behave. And that means that I have shape-shifted, and I have been co-opted, and I have been beaten down—*all* of the things I mentioned, not just one of them. I've been through the forge, and I now resemble a corporate citizen.

Vic: Resemble. Does that mean that at heart you are not? That it's a facade? That you've taken on the coloration? Or have you become one?

Beth: To a certain extent I have changed. And to a certain extent I'm just playing my role. I'm somebody who follows the rules, and the rules are very strong and clear here. But my value system hasn't changed too much. I've got to revise that. It has changed quite a bit.

Vic: Talk about your value system, your core values. How have they changed? What are they now? What were they before? Can you comment on that?

Beth: No. Not necessarily. Through talking with you maybe I can. I know my ten commandments, but I don't know my ten core values. I haven't sat down and articulated them.

On Being a Team Player

Beth: What has shifted for me are my assumptions about the place of money and power in the corporate world. I hadn't been aware of how powerful the corporate world is and what a powerful force money is in driving behavior.

What has remained constant are my assumptions about being a team player and winning. Once I'm in a game, I want to win, whether I ever thought I wanted to play the game or not. So if you put me on a baseball team, I'll be a very aggressive player toward winning for our team—even though I don't care about baseball and don't voluntarily run down to the park and play. It isn't my activity of choice. But if I'm on a team, I become an enthusiastic team player. And that's what's happened to me.

So this is my home team, this is what we're trying to

achieve, and damn! I'm going to try my hardest to see that we achieve it! And that's a core value.

Vic: Can you look a little behind your being an enthusiastic player and having that commitment? What assumption drives you in that? Do you know?

Beth: I think because it's fun when you're a team player. I enjoy the camaraderie. As somebody who comes from a large family—although people from large families can become isolationist—I respond to it with feeling comfortable working together toward a goal. Whether it's a baseball team or a corporate target or Habitat for Humanity—whatever the project—I enjoy being part of a team or beehive that's working toward something. The warmth of that feels like a naturally comfortable place for me.

There is also a core belief that as part of a team I should be treated fairly and that the team should be rewarded. But in our culture, while it has this team mentality, it also has a star mentality. You've got football teams and baseball teams and soccer teams, but only one or two people are singled out to be stars. The rest are simply the ants or the proletariat that are there to allow the stars to shine. And people generally don't recognize the interdependency of all the team members and that the star couldn't run around the ball field if there weren't people in position at every base.

Vic: Are you not a star?

Beth: I don't feel like a star in my corporate culture. I'm more of a star outside of my corporation. My field recognizes me, but I still don't feel that my corporation recognizes me. I haven't been designated as one of the stars by my company. People not at the level of management I've gotten to would say, "Gosh, you've gotten that far, you're a star." But when I look at the inner circle, I don't feel like a star.

Vic: So it depends on which circle you're looking at. If you look at the right circle, you're a star; if you look at the wrong circle, you're a loser.

Beth: Right.

Vic: In that sense, since the circles go on infinitely . . .

Beth: Why not pick the one with which you can feel good about yourself?

Vic: That's a wonderful question. But how important is it to you that you continue to strive in the circle where you don't see yourself as a star? Is your dissatisfaction with "*I am not a star in every circle*" what's driving you?

Beth: I don't know. To unpack it would require more discussion. To put it in a suitcase that I use a lot, I can say: *I have a very strong work ethic.* My Hawaiian name means *One who is willing to do the work.* And I am by nature a hard worker. Now there are probably a lot of assumptions behind all of that . . .

Vic: . . . going back to your Catholic upbringing.

Beth: Catholic school was major.

Machine-Gun Merle and Other Teachers

Vic: What was the nickname of the Sister who was your teacher?

Beth: *Atom Bomb.* Sister Anita Bernerd. *Machine-Gun Merle* was another. That was Sister Mary Martina. They all had affectionate names like that, related to their gentle natures.

Vic: You grew up in a very demanding school of performance.

Beth: I feel as if I had been in a military academy. It was very strict, very tough. It wasn't about a kinder, gentler society; it was about *Toe the line, and here it is!*

Vic: Yet you are probably one of the most gentle people I know— philosophically, in terms of your values. In the corporate world, do you show a different aspect of yourself?

Beth: Even in the corporate world I'm that way. Which makes my relative success all the more astounding. No wonder I'm so tired.

Vic: Talk about that.

Beth: I hear people in my industry stand up and say things like, *Beth is really a gentle leader, a quiet leader,* compared to most of my peers who grandstand and talk loudly and animatedly and really dramatically at all times, and who jockey for space and recognition. Someone else said about my leadership, *Yes, Beth just sits there and she listens and she observes and she thinks about things, but when she has something to say, POW!*

But I really do feel like a stranger in a strange land. And I feel that, as a stranger, I've been relatively successful, given that I am *not* the profile of what is successful in Corporate America.

Vic: You may be the profile of what Corporate America really needs to be successful in this changing, emerging world.

Beth: When I look back at law school, I feel I've been a woman who has been able to survive this foreign environment and bring myself and my values to bear. Which isn't always comfortable for me, and it's not always comfortable for the dominant culture. But I think—and here we get back to diversity—to the extent that people who are different can tolerate staying within a different culture and that culture can tolerate them, the culture and they are richer.

Diversity and the Fertile Crescent

Beth: I heard a wonderful speech by Buddy McKay, former governor of Florida and now United States Economic Ambassador to the Americas. He talked of how diversity is so valuable in biological ecosystems and how they call the area that is the most rich and has the most diversity *The Edge* because it's where two different ecosystems come together. Where they meet is the most rich, the most lush, the most fertile, the most productive, the most diverse.

The analogy carries over to other environments. Where that edge exists—the intersection between different ways of thought, different ways of being—there you have the potential and possibility for so much more. If you protect and honor that edge, rather than try to build Berlin Walls or hard divides, then it becomes the Fertile Crescent. You have the chance to see what can evolve from there that is new and different, to see the combinations of ideas and everything else that would never have occurred in a distinct culture of some sort.

I think we have some inspiring times and some very scary times ahead with globalization. The fear is that the dominant culture will take over everything and wipe out differentness and uniqueness. That will be a great loss on many levels. Pretty soon we won't be able to have the unique experience travel offers: different language, different currency, different foods, different smells, different sounds. Everyone will be speaking English, eating at McDonald's and using the Euro as their currency. It will no longer be: *Oh gee! Look at this giant French franc. Isn't it neat? It doesn't fit in my wallet, it has beautiful watermarks, and all these pictures of people from French history.*

I've always loved that about travel—seeing the world from so many different perspectives.

The exciting part is that we're getting more intersections of cultures than ever before. In the past, people who worked for the United Nations or for the diplomatic corps or an international organization almost always ended up taking a few years back at home for R and R because it can be very tiring to be different from your surrounding culture all the time. It can be exciting and energizing, but there's also a need to return to your native state and not having to deal with all the differentness that's facing you. I don't know how that will change in a more homogenized world.

Emotional Expression in the Corporate World

Vic: You mentioned earlier that one of the sociologists from the university was saying you're not expected to express emotion in corporate culture. Do you agree with the sociologist's judgment?

Beth: Yes, I do. Emotions—particularly great happiness or great sadness or extreme emotions like that—are inappropriate. Also, when they are expressed, they aren't acknowledged and responded to or used in a fruitful way.

Vic: What assumptions are at work here?

Beth: The assumption of corporate culture is that deviancy costs time and money. That the more things are the same—the less perturbations in the wave, the less oscillation, the more steady state—the more things will move ahead faster.

Vic: Isn't that contrary to corporations becoming more and more responsive to the needs for diversity?

Beth: I think it's very challenging and difficult for corporations to honor diversity.

Vic: Because it doesn't allow itself to have a heart? Or emotion?

Beth: It all has to do with money. Corporations are focused on short-term gain. Diversity leads to longer-term gain but I don't think it leads to shorter-term gain.

You want people to stay *"Nose to the grindstone," "Focus on four key deliverables,"* and that's it. And if they're laughing or they're crying, that's 20 minutes that they might be spending on doing the spreadsheets. You want people to be flying like geese in the wind. Nobody is one micrometer off from their place in the chevron, because if they are, then the team will go slower. If there is one goose back there going, "Lah la lah" and flapping around, then the chevron is not advancing as quickly through the wind. And that's how the corporation views it. Similarly, incorporating diversity from a short-term perspective loses time and money.

Vic: Is that good or bad?

Beth: It's good if your goal is to increase your immediate profitability. It's bad if your goal is to promote diversity and develop long-term growth and profitability.

Vic: So your goals for diversity—your job as a promoter of diversity in the corporate world—run counter to the corporation's need to limit diversity and increase profitability.

Beth: Yes, but the corporation can accept diversity to a certain degree on many levels—such as gender and ethnicity—but you may not have diversity on the performance level.

Vic: Like, *You're in the Army, you better wear the uniform properly and say Yes Sir, No Sir . . .*

Beth: Yes. You can be white, black, brown or yellow, but you behave by the rules.

I started with the assumption that I and my cohort could effect change. Now, I still think we can, but it's a long process. And things are moving so rapidly in our society right now. They have accelerated to an incredible pitch. Even if you're trying to avoid it. But to be in the middle of it as I am, in an information-technology industry that is changing more rapidly than anything else, I feel as if I'm going at warp speed in a company that's in the major-league playoffs.

In another time we might have been a different kind of culture, but now it's *'All hands on deck!'* It's not only, *'You're in the Navy now,'* it's *'All hands on deck!'* We're now at war in the fever pitch of battle; the winner will survive and the loser will not. So it's demanding that kind of dedication.

Vic: Sounds thrilling.

Beth: Right. It is. And that's part of what keeps me going too.

I think the assumptions you can get down to are: *We are at war. This is real. This is not an exercise or a playtime.* And for the corporate world, this is very real. I do think the biochemistry is a large part of what keeps people going—the adrenaline rush that is so addictive. Keeping folks in a state of urgency and fervor that attaches to being in a state of war is what keeps them hooked into high-powered performance month after month.

Personal Cost and Sacrifice

Vic: Can you talk about the costs involved in being a player, for you personally?

Beth: Yes. It's fun to be on a great soccer team, but you've got to be in good condition and completely devoted—and there are all the sacrifices. The notorious impact of military life on the family also applies at the higher levels of corporate life. That is one of the major problems for me. When it's time to play ball, I am 100 percent there. But when I change settings, I'm camping or out in nature, for example, I'm experiencing a shift in perspective and I say, *Gosh, there's a lovely meditation spot over there,* and I look around and see that life contains all these other things that I cannot be involved in.

Oh, there are plenty of people in corporate culture who are doing a lot of those other things, but they're not in the thick of the game if they are. My boss works seven days a week, 18 to 20 hours a day, day in and day out.

Vic: Does he appear to be enjoying it?

Beth: Yes, he does. Because if you're a player, you see yourself as one, and you say, *I'm in this game!*

Of course, to be a big player you need lots of behind-the-scenes support from others. My boss and his wife have jointly decided that he gets to be a leader. He gets to call the plays, and he's the quarterback on the team. They decided that it's a great opportunity not to be passed by. Just as Irish Catholic families used to designate one out of ten of their children to the religious life, he is designated to go to *The Game,* and everybody in his system supports him by taking care of their personal lives, the children, the social ties, and everything else. They all benefit from his being a star player and get hugely rewarded financially, and they consider the quid pro quo worth it.

Not to mention that once you get to be a player, it's pretty hard to let go of it—the adrenaline, the excitement.

Vic: I assume that someday you hope to be in a position where the adrenaline will not be flowing quite so much. Is that a correct assumption?

Beth: I don't know. I think that's the other thing about me: I'm relatively easily excited. And I engage quickly. I'm not on the sidelines. I'm excited by a lot of things that other people wouldn't find exciting. It's all fun to me. I don't have to be an important person on the playing field to be excited. I don't have to be in the corporate games to be thrilled.

Vic: Life is exciting for you.

Beth: Yes. Life is exciting, and any number of things that are happening in life are exciting.

Vic: That's such a wonderful gift to be that way.

Beth: It really is.

Vic: How did this gift get nurtured in you?

Beth: I don't know. A simple pat answer is that it's my nature cultivated over many lifetimes. But I do appreciate it. And I sure would want that for Tracy, and I see that Tracy has that gift.

Vic: Do you have to take care of it? Nurture it? Or does it just bubble up so much that it doesn't take any conscious attention?

Beth: When I'm really tired and down, it doesn't manifest. But what I find is that beneath the surface, it's always there. Like, *Hope springs eternal,* it's there. It's very resilient.

Vic: What would you say to people who don't have this gift of *joie de vivre*?

Beth: I would recommend spending time with children. It's fun to share learning to read with Tracy, and I'm enjoying the process of seeing it happen. I don't want to miss out on that.

I would recommend spending quite a bit of time in nature, by oneself. I look on being at one with nature as our natural state and a gift from God.

I do think you can cultivate a good life and enjoy things by being around people who are very positive and active in nature, walks by the river, camping. It's a lot easier if you are doing all those things and are supported and loved than it is if you are beleaguered.

The Core Dilemma: Am I Serving God or Mammon?

Beth: Okay—Now we're getting into this whole thing of "What am I doing there?" Am I endangering my mortal soul? Or am I studying with my Zen Master? Is this all grist for the mill that's going to help me evolve and become united with the One, manifesting One? Or am I squandering and destroying the blessings that I've been given?

Vic: That has been an issue for you from the very beginning, has it not?

Beth: Yes. It's my koan. But whatever the answers to those questions are, it isn't that I am committed to 100 percent dedication to the corporate games. They're like the Olympic Games. I look at Michele Kwan, I look at my Olympic idols, and I'm very impressed. I didn't go for that kind of excellence, but I find myself on a team that's saying, *Well, we're in the Olympics, and if you want to stay on the team, you darn well better practice 18 hours a day like the rest of us!* And I say, *O.K. I don't want to be the one to cause the team to lose, and I did sign on, and if I'm here, I should be toeing the line. That's only fair.*

On the other hand, as I sit here and listen to Tracy and watch her learn to spell and how to make friends, *There's No Way!* This is as important, or more important. So it's difficult trying to find balance and diversity in my own life in a system that by definition says, *Diversity is failure.*

Vic: Isn't that the answer to your question, *Am I endangering my mortal soul or studying with my Zen Master?*—this finding of an internal balance so that your own life is whole, so that you are serving both God and Mammon, in a sense.

Beth: Yes. On the one hand, I am committed to the path of spiritual liberation. I do believe that we are here for a purpose. I'm here to know, love and serve God. It's the same catechism I studied as a child in Catholic school, that I was born to love and serve God. That's one unshakable assumption for me. That's my core assumption.

On the other hand, I do believe that you could still be following that path and devote yourself to the corporate games—if you were able to be a spiritual master or just a very skillful student. Otherwise, the tendency is to get lost and reach the end of your life going, *Oh my God, What did I do? How did I get so far off course?*

Part of the spiritual path, from my perspective, is helping all beings attain enlightenment. People who can come with some level of consciousness into the corporate culture are not going to transform it in any kind of dramatic way in short order. But I think that just having somebody in that environment hold you in a different regard and not view you as replaceable goods in the goal of winning the game, can be very helpful. And to the extent that more and more people can come into the corporate culture who hold values that people are worth more than what they produce and that diversity is important, the hope is that you are working toward the enlightenment of all beings.

If you're having a hellish day, a minimum-wage cashier in the cafeteria who treats you with loving kindness as you go through her line can give you a moment of salvation in a day of hell. She's a ray of light. It doesn't matter where you are or what your role is. There are also people in more powerful roles who can do that.

Missionaries in the Corporate World

Beth: I look at what percentage of the population spend their days in this environment and how we all need a little help from our friends. It's important, I think, to have outreach programs that provide the humor and the blessings that one can give to other people during the day. One of my more enjoyable moments at MegaMega—where some seven thousand of us worked in the same building—was when people were talking about printing up bumper stickers that would read: *Free the MegaMega 7,000!*

Vic: Not the Chicago Seven.

Beth: Right.

Vic: That's wonderful.

Beth: You know, we have people who go out and do missionary work in the Tenderloin and in prisons. I think evangelical work is needed in corporate office buildings. People outside playing wind chimes or harps, so that when you enter and exit, your mind is taken to a slightly different place and you are reminded that you are more than a productive employee. That could be refreshing. Of course, if you were trespassing on corporate premises, you'd probably be arrested.

Vic: Hang wind chimes from the trees.

Beth: Yeah, when I first came there I tried to do stuff like that. A fast way to get fired. But seriously, if I were running a corporation, I would look for ways to bring in light.

For example, if there were massage chairs and everybody got one ticket a month to use whenever they wanted and they could come in for a 15-minute back-and-neck massage. Little things like that to give people an acknowledgment that there is more to them and more to life. And while the quid pro quo is clear here—it's ten hours of your undivided attention for x days a week and in exchange you get these things, that's the contract—and also, because we honor that you are more than this, we're going to give you these extras, like 15-minute massages each month.

But in the minds of most of those who run things now, those extras would take away from corporate productivity. I tend to think the extras would enhance it. Experiments and studies would have to statistically prove the benefit before most corporations would even consider such a notion. Unfortunately, even when statistically valid research proves that an unorthodox practice—such as job sharing—will benefit the corporation, it is still too difficult for the corporation to accept.

Vic: Are there corporations that are taking a more humanistic view?

Beth: I don't really know. A lot of them say they are, but I know people in some of those corporations, and it's not true at all. This is either part of their self-delusion or self-promotion, or both. I did see a television program about a software company in North Carolina that went to a 35-hour work week. The owner got on television and said that he doesn't think that programmers do good work after a certain amount of time; that's where you get the bugs in a program, and it's far more expensive to do the rework. He said he believes he has been able to prove unequivocally that the shorter work week is more cost-effective for him.

So there may be some like that.

Because there are so many of us in corporate culture and because it is a social form of life, it would be incredible to take a corporation through a next level of evolution, where it could be a winner. Right now there's a belief, a corporate assumption that to be humanistic is one big joke! You either kick butt and win, or you have a more humanistic view and you lose. But instead of saying, *We're going to voluntarily self-destruct in order to acknowledge the humanity of our members,* it could be a company that says, *We're still going to be Number One, and we're going to do this too.*

Vic: Sounds to me like you have just prepared your Personal Mission Statement.

The Need for Sacred Time

Vic: For the record, you were mentioning before how the stock market is going 24 hours a day now and pointing to that as indicative of how rapidly things are changing and how dehumanizing it is. How it has to be recognized that people need to have human time.

Beth: And that's what Shabbat (Sabbath) is about. Shabbat declares that not all human time can be conscripted. Shabbat is sacred and inviolable. Into the religious rules and scriptures of Judaism, they created this period of time. Then Christian tradition followed with Sunday. On Sundays, the blue laws: no alcohol, etc. Now the doors of corporate business are open 24 hours a day, seven days a week—there is no sacred time. With Shabbat or sacred time, no matter how you choose to use that time, it's noncommercial time.

From Judaism's perspective, human beings are not looked at merely as beasts of burden or production units. The immortal soul needs to be acknowledged and given its due. If you don't carve out time for that and acknowledge it, not just as a thought but in life, then you don't have anything.

Vic: Your boss and the corporate world that he is totally absorbed in is in violation of that.

Beth: Total violation. There is no sacred space. To them, *Work is a god.* It is a religion.

Things are happening at many different levels, and you can apply a lot of different metaphors and analogies to explore it. In the 19th century women and children worked 14-hour days at the factory, so it's not that this is the most ungodly time compared to others, but I think there are risks of being dangerously out of balance if we don't pay more attention.

My company asserts: *We support volunteerism. We support people's involvement in the community.* People can espouse volunteerism but the bottom line is, if you aren't afforded time to do it, it doesn't happen. It's an age-old struggle.

Vic: The Jews came up with the idea of Sabbath 5,000 years ago.

Beth: In this country the employees' only break was Sunday. But thank God it was there, and it's only because of religion. God trumped the CEOs.

Vic: And, in a sense, now the CEOs are trumping God.

Beth: That's right. There's no Sabbath and no Sunday anymore.

Vic: So it's time for something different.

Beth: A lot of people think, *Well sure, that's good in theory, but if I have my production unit functioning less than my competitor's pro-*

duction unit, etc. There has to be a pact, a truce, where we'd all agree to lay down arms for 24 hours a week or whatever it is.

Vic: You pointed out that corporate life provides a lot of stimulation and excitement and energy. What's missing, if I understand you correctly, is a balance between excitement of competition and renewal.

Beth: Not just renewal but the feeling and caring and nurturing of other aspects of life—the life of music, the arts, politics, education, community service—all of those lives and not just renewal from the corporate life.

WHAT TO DO ABOUT THEM

Beth Cameron makes the following assumptions about the corporate world—and about herself as a corporate citizen. Consider how her assumptions compare with your own? And in what ways?

- *Corporate America has a strong culture of its own that demands all members, no matter their diverse backgrounds, diverse thought processes, diverse genders, diverse ethnicities, diverse ways of thinking, to conform to the corporate culture's model for ways of being in the world.*
- *If I'm on a team, I become an enthusiastic team player. And that's what's happened to me. This is my home team, this is what we're trying to achieve, and damn! I'm going to try my hardest to see that we achieve it! And that's a core value.*
- *An assumption of the corporate culture is that deviancy costs time and money. That the more things are the same, the less perturbations in the wave, the less oscillation, the more steady state there is, things will move ahead faster.*
- *Corporate core assumptions are: We are at war. This is real. This is not an exercise or a playtime. And for the corporate world, this is very real.*
- *There's a corporate assumption that you either kick butt and win, or you have a more humanistic view and you lose.*

Notes & Comments

Notes & Comments

Notes & Comments

12

Making It in Small Business

Conversation with Bruce Milletto

Topic Index

12

Making It in Small Business

Conversation with Bruce Milletto

Vic: I'd like you to talk about your beliefs, your assumptions concerning what makes for success and failure in the world of small business.

Bruce: First of all, I see business as a chess game, so I've trained myself to think ahead about the third or fourth move, not the move I'm making right now. And, as in a chess match, in business I have to make numerous assumptions daily about my competition and market.

Many business owners don't equate chess with business and are unable to operate and make decisions in this manner. It's a gift if they're able to do that.

On Becoming a Business Chess Player

Vic: Do you understand how you came by this gift, this ability to think two or three moves ahead? Was it through your experience in business or something you learned earlier?

Bruce: I learned much of this from having to be street-smart to survive. I've always considered myself fortunate to have grown up without realizing, until I was a freshman in college, that I grew up rather poor. The second day of college, in Psychology

101, we were studying about the poverty level in the United States. I knew what my parents' combined income was, but only at that moment did I learn that we were about 20 percent below the poverty level in the United States.

I was shocked. Although my parents never bought a new car, never owned their own home, I always had the nice clothes and usually had the spending money I needed, partially because I held down one or more part-time jobs from about age ten.

I believe that getting to where I am now—having success in most endeavors—came from my upbringing and was a gift from my parents. When I wanted a tape recorder in junior high school, my parents took me down to the Firestone store and asked the owner if I could pay off the tape recorder at five dollars a week. From an early age I think I truly understood the value of money and the value of work. Experiences such as this and growing up as an only child made me somewhat savvy about survival.

I've considered—assumed—it was a blessing that I never received a dime from my parents since I was 17 years old. I paid for my own college, my first house, cars, insurance. And while there were times I felt slighted, for the most part I felt grateful.

A Glass Half Full

Vic: So you made the assumption that you were blessed by hardship rather than that you were a deprived child.

Bruce: I really looked at having to work as a fortunate experience. It's all in how you perceive that.

In college, I was one of eight friends in a dormitory. The other seven had parents who paid for their tuition and room and board and a car, and possibly sent them $100 a week. There were two ways I could have dealt with the disparity between their situations and my own. I could have said, *I've been screwed. Why me?* Or I could say, *Where does the advantage lie here?* It's "the glass is half full or the glass is half empty" scenario. I chose to see it as the glass half full. I won't lie and say that every moment of my life I felt that way, but in general I have.

Vic: So you are basically an optimist and tend to see things positively.

Bruce: Yes. In most situations I grasp for the positive, no matter how negative things might be. I'll think, *What advantages are there in this negative experience? What have I learned? What may come out of it that would be positive?* Often I try to focus on one positive point rather than on all the negative points in a particular situation.

You Can Do It!—Usually

Vic: You're making a lot of assumptions having to do with beliefs that where there's a will, there's a way, that making positive choices is better than making negative choices, and that it's better to see the glass half full than half empty. How do all of these assumptions work out in the world of business?

Bruce: I really believe that people can do just about anything they want to do. But many people I come in contact with in business seem to look only at the small picture of what life has to offer.

Yesterday morning I was on the phone with two of the owners of a firm similar to mine. They provide educational materials, as we do. When they came out with a product that appeared to be somewhat competitive, it got my attention. As I thought about this product's impact on my company, I came to the conclusion that joining them and striking a strategic alliance might be better than assuming we had to be direct competitors. I called them to hammer out the basis of a potential contractual agreement.

It seemed to me they kept focusing on the smaller picture:

What would the alliance do for us today and next week and next month? And while that's important, I had been looking at a bigger picture: In general, our two firms play to different audiences, so on a large scale, we're not in competition. We have products that could be compatible and help sales on both sides. In the bigger picture beyond next week and next month, we possibly could do many things together to cut our expenses and support each other. For example, we could market together, do trade shows together, share data bases, and involve each other's firms in complex consulting situations, with each of us bringing our particular strengths to a client.

Vic: You emphasize the vital importance of a larger vision and believe that collaboration can be more advantageous than competition. Do you think most small businesses fail to generate a larger vision?

Bruce: I wouldn't use the word *most,* but I would say that many small businesses fail to realize potential. They often fail or struggle because they're not visionary.

With Bellissimo we have a business that is unique in the entire world. And it's unique because we've held to a larger vision.

A few years back I was sitting in a piazza in Italy with a good friend who asked me, *Who's your competition? Who else does what you do?* And it was at that point I realized that no one else in the world does what we do. If you're an attorney or a hairdresser or a legal secretary or a broom maker, there are others on the planet who do the same job you do. We occupy a very small niche. We saw a need and filled it quickly. We became the standard-bearer for an industry and for clients who needed information and educational materials about coffee.

Along the way we were tempted by a number of small-picture offers. For example, at a time when we were in a small office and anxious to move, one coffee-equipment dealer offered to rent us office space and help us with the rent for three years. But we didn't bite on that hook because in the big picture we would always be seen as being in bed with this company. *Oh sure, Bellissimo, they do educational products but they're really tied to XYZ company.*

Skateboarding in Traffic

Vic: What differences do you see between running a small firm like Bellissimo and being the CEO of a large corporation like Starbucks?

Bruce: I wrote an article in a trade journal a while back on how a single-unit coffee bar could compete with a large chain, and I used an example that came to me while riding in a cab through heavy Seattle traffic. As we moved fitfully in stop-and-go fashion, I saw a teenager on a skateboard flying down the sidewalk. He got to the bottom of the hill three times as fast as my cab and probably six times as fast as a large truck.

I often see the coffee chain as a large truck.

The chain has certain advantages if there's a complete roadblock. They may have staff attorneys and power the small operator does not. But the small owner, like the skateboard, may be able to maneuver quickly or stop on a dime. Change does not require a committee. I see this as a huge advantage at times.

Many small-business people make the assumption they can't compete with a large chain. But I believe they have many advantages over the chain. In the consulting part of our business I explain the positive side of tighter controls, quicker decisions and usually a better product with better customer service. Small can be beautiful.

In my business, I often make a decision for Bellissimo in three minutes that would get bogged down in committee for a year or two in the large corporation. I don't have the luxury of taking three months or a year to make a decision. This so-called luxury may be counterproductive in a large business. Small business, on the other hand, is about speed, flexibility, quick thinking and risk-taking.

Another advantage of a small business is that the staff is usually more fully integrated into the operation of the business, apprised of what's going on and more involved in the decision-making process. In a large corporation the organization chart is made up of boxes on top of other boxes, and employees are pigeon-holed and distanced from most of the process. Once you accomplish A, B and C, you're done. But small business is about taking risks on a daily basis. It's about rocking the boat and sometimes getting wet while you're pinpointing the spot on the horizon you are navigating towards.

Balancing Business and Marriage

Vic: One of the traditional thorny thickets for married couples arises from the impact on our marriages of the assumptions we make in our business lives. Can you talk about the demands of your business life and their impact on your marriage? Is it possible to live happily in both places?

Bruce: I think it is. But the more successful you are in business, the more of a challenge it is, with long hours and stressors that a nine-to-five employee in a large corporation cannot imagine. In successful businesses, extensive travel is often required. Having to make three major trips to different parts of the world in a matter of two months, as happened to me recently, can put a lot of strain on a marriage and can create some major challenges.

One of the first jobs I had after college was travelling and teaching for the National Endowment for the Arts. I was on the road for about 12 days and home two, and I can remember coming back to my home and finding myself in an alien atmosphere. I was used to staying up as late as I wanted and going out and doing whatever I wanted. My wife was used to the same thing. It was uncomfortable for her when I came home because she had gotten into a routine that worked for her. Being on the road, I had done the same thing. These types of adjustments can be difficult.

But I think it all depends on how strong the relationship is. How much love is there? How hard do both of you want to try? There needs to be that deep-seated love and commitment to overcome the challenges. If there's enough love, people can live on the other side of the earth and work 80 hours a week and maintain a relationship.

Vic: If the communication and commitment are there.

Bruce: Yes.

Balancing Business and Children

Vic: How about the impact of your business life on your relationships with your children?

Bruce: I've been able to take advantage of my need to travel on business to develop special relationships with my children. I took both of my children to Europe because I believed it would be the most important educational experience I could give them. First, I took Mathew for five weeks when he was ten. I really couldn't afford it, but from a bonding standpoint I felt it was very important that he and I have that one-on-one time together and have that adventure and face that challenge together.

As one way of having fun and learning from one another, I had Mathew keep track of our budget every day, how much we had to spend—X for hotel, Y for transportation, Z for food, and then a miscellaneous category that we were allowed to spend every day. At the end of each day, in our hotel room, we would take ten minutes to balance the books. So, in a sense, we ran a little business while we traveled. I believe it was the best five weeks the two of us could have spent together.

Vic: What a marvelous experience for the two of you. Where is Mathew now, and what is he doing?

Bruce: He's in school in Italy. Part of what that earlier experience accomplished was to open his eyes to the rest of the world. He also traveled with me to other countries.

Getting from A to C

Vic: I'm impressed with the way you made room for Mathew on various trips and used it to further his education and provide him with a role model. Can you cite other instances where you were able to do that?

Bruce: Yes. I can think of another involving Mathew and still another, involving Whitney, my daughter.

When Mathew was in the second grade, my wife and I took him on a seven-week trip throughout the South Pacific, and I found a way of putting him in school on various islands. In Rarotonga I went to the school district and said, *How would it be possible to allow my son to attend school here?* Their first response was, *Oh my, no. The rules do not permit this.* And I said, *But there must be some way. I have teaching credentials. What if I come in and teach for two days as a trade for allowing him to go to school for one week?* And the response was, *Well, that's an interesting idea.*

It worked. And I remember Mathew coming home at night and telling us that at recess he and one of his little friends went out in a dugout canoe and speared fish.

Vic: That's a creative solution.

Bruce: The second one that comes to mind takes a little longer to tell.

When Whitney, who is 13 now, turned ten, she and I went to Europe for a little over three weeks. There are times when Mathew and I think more alike than Whitney and I do, in that he and I tend to see the glass as half full. Whitney at times leans a bit more toward seeing the glass as half empty, and this became strikingly clear when the two of us were by ourselves in Italy.

We were in the little town of Positano. Over dinner one

evening we found out that Ray Charles would be playing down on the beach where we had noticed a large stage. Even more attractive for me, since I'm not a great Ray Charles fan, was the fact that some Italian groups would also be playing. Then I found out that because of the limited seating at this very small venue, the tickets were about $100 each .

On that particular trip, I was writing three articles for three separate magazines. One of the magazines, *Italian Journal of Food, Wine & Travel,* wanted me to do a piece on Positano, and I saw the Ray Charles concert as fitting in. You know—*A concert such as this is one of the things that happens in Positano in the summertime . . .* It made sense to me that I needed to be at this concert and that I shouldn't have to pay to get in, because my writing would promote Positano as a tourist destination.

I said to Whitney, *Tomorrow morning we're going to see what we can work out about attending this concert tomorrow night.* And Whitney said, *Dad, we can't go to that concert, it's $100 a ticket!* So I said, *Let's just see what the possibilities are. Maybe we'll pay nothing.*

I decided to approach what is the equivalent of the Positano Chamber of Commerce, and their response was: *We don't know . . . you need to go talk to Angelica . . . and Angelica is at such-and-such hotel, but she's not there until five o'clock tonight . . .* and so forth.

I got a huge runaround. I talked to three or four people and got nowhere. So after one of these deadends Whitney said, *Dad, this is not going to work!* And I said, *Whitney, I want you to watch how it is going to work.* And she looked at me and asked, *How do you know?* And I said, *Because I believe it. I just believe in myself to make it work.*

We ate breakfast and went shopping and went to the beach. And that afternoon on the beach I said to her: *We need to get back to the pensione early tonight because I want to get showered and go downtown early to find Angelica who, supposedly, is the key to our getting tickets.*

She was out of her lounge chair and sitting on the pebbly beach, and she again said to me, *Dad, just give it up. They pretty much told you "No" this morning.*

So I said to Whitney, *I want to show you something.*

Then I placed two very shiny white rocks across from each other on the pebbly beach, and I said, *In life, most people think that you get from this rock to this rock like this:* And I drew a straight line between the two white rocks. *But in most cases in life, that's never the way it works. First, you have to go over to this rock on the right, then over to this rock on the left, then maybe go back to that same rock on the right, and then hop over here, and back and forth and back and forth, and then, finally, you get to this other white rock. And that's the way life works.*

And that's what we're going through right now. We're hopping from rock to rock to rock to try to get to that white rock on the other side. And if you look at life like, "If I can't drive straight to that other rock, then I don't want to go," then you'll probably never get to the rock you want to be on.

And I saw this little ten-year-old mind taking it in, but she still wasn't convinced.

That night at the Chamber of Commerce, two hours before the concert started, things were even twice as negative and 100 times more chaotic. And it was at this point that Whitney was able to observe firsthand our rock analogy. With her at my side in the crowded room, I finally announced: *This is ridiculous! I have looked for this Angelica; she is not available. I have been over to the site four times. This is totally crazy. I deserve and want a press pass, and I want it right now!*

And they said, *Okay, Okay.* And they gave it to me. And then I said, *This will also admit my daughter?* And they said *Oh, no no no—this is only for you.* And I said, *Excuse me, my daughter is ten years old, she's with me, and I obviously need a pass for her too.* And we got one.

And I will never forget the look on Whitney's face as we came out of that office with passes that said, "Press."

She said, *Dad, you were right! I can't believe this. You really made this happen!*

I've thought often of that instance and a dozen others that weren't necessarily positive at the time. Those were equally as important learning experiences as time spent looking at 1,000-year-old churches. Often they are the lessons that help us navigate life.

Right Brain/Left Brain

Vic: I want to go to a different topic. I see you as being uniquely involved in two worlds: the artistic world and the world of business. How important is it to have both of these temperaments—the creative artistic and the rationally practical—if you're going to be successful as a small businessman?

Bruce: I believe that few people really have the mentality to be an entrepreneur. Background experience and how one's thought processes work, I believe, are key. Success or failure as an entrepreneur in small- or medium-sized business is in direct correlation with, and often determined by, one's attitude and thought processes.

If you look at a business from strictly a logical, analytical viewpoint, you are using a left-brain approach. A right-brain approach is looking at it from an artistic standpoint. I think that the more a person is both right- and left-brained, the more successful he or she will be in starting and running a business.

I remember one of my first jobs when I worked for Motorola Semi-Conductor Products Division in Phoenix, Arizona. I was 19 and had taken a year off from college. This is a gigantic plant with thousands of employees. I often slipped suggestions into the suggestion box in the hallway—ideas for improvements that I kept seeing. Every week they would put out a newsletter and offer $50 for the best suggestion. I believe I won that about ten times in one year. If you think creatively in this way, then you may be in the wrong business if you're working for someone else. Creative yet analytical thinkers may do well in an entrepreneurial atmosphere.

In another situation, I was the director of an art center, and I was dealing with predominantly right-brain people. When I took over the directorship, there were myriad major problems, many of which were hidden ones that the former director had created. On my second day on the job, I found out that we had over $60,000 in 30-, 60- and 90-day payables, and when I looked at the checkbook, we had only $600 in our account.

So over the next two or three years that I was the director, I needed to figure out ways to get from that one white rock to the next white rock. If ever there was an example that there's no straight line from one to the next, this was it.

One important thing is that the rocks I chose to hop onto were rocks of friendship and rocks of understanding. I had to explain to Pepsi-Cola, to whom we owed a large sum from an art event, that there was no way we could pay the entire sum given our dilemma. But we did want to pay them something and wanted to work out a payment schedule. We weren't saying, *You'll never get your money*, but, *How much of that will you write off for us?* We cut that invoice down by two-thirds and started to make $200-a-month payments on the balance. At least we were making an attempt.

Housed in the art center were print-making, ceramics and painting cooperatives. Unfortunately, all of them were alienated from the center and were taking advantage of it by not paying their bills. The financial reality was that the center's back taxes had not been paid. The IRS had served notice and within 90 days planned to lock our doors. If this happened, nobody would have anything. I wouldn't have my job, and they wouldn't have their studios to do their work.

So, getting back to considerations of right and left brain, I remember vividly the day I sat in my office and brought in representatives from the different cooperatives and tried to explain the situation to them. After an hour of talking, it was clear that they didn't understand any of it. For them, it didn't compute. At which point I opened up my desk drawer and I pulled out the checkbook and the financial statements.

I thought that once they saw the debts we had incurred—that I had inherited—they'd understand that the only way to continue working would be to contribute their fair share and not take a handout from the center.

It was a moment I'll never forget. They looked at what I had presented, and they still didn't understand.

So while having a highly developed right-brain aptitude is helpful in business, if you have only that—as the members of the co-op had on that memorable day—you're never going to be successful.

Playing the Devil

Vic: I'm curious. How did you deal with that situation?

Bruce: I became the devil. It was the only costume I could wear. I took an art center that could barely afford my salary—which was peanuts—and cut the staff by about two-thirds. That created major problems because no one could understand how the former director could have a staff of eight or nine people and I couldn't afford more than two or three. And how would I *dare* fire these people? But the hard reality was that the previous director couldn't afford it either, and he was robbing Peter to pay Paul.

We had a number of galleries and a gift shop. We took 33 percent of the gift-shop sales, and the artist received the remainder. But there was never money to pay the artist, and I had artists calling me every day and saying, *I sold a $2,000 neon sculpture six months ago, and I still haven't received my commission check!* So where does the center come up with $1,300 today to make a commission payment? The money had been spent on staff.

Coming from an art background myself, I have incredible sympathy for the artist who put in the time and energy to create this product and hasn't been paid for it. He's been robbed, his money has been used to keep the art center open, but that isn't his responsibility. Bringing up this problem to the board of directors, I said: *What needs to happen is simple. We need to have two accounts. At the end of the day we need to deposit one-third of the money in our account and deposit two-thirds of the money in a savings account, so at the end of month we can pay our artists.*

And here I have a board of directors made up of professional people, and they respond with, *You're a genius! What a brilliant idea!* But it's absolutely the most common-sense idea that ever was.

It's a Juggle Out There

Bruce: It is no different in the business I now own and run. There is no lack of project ideas for a business like Bellissimo, but you have to be able to maintain cash flow to operate safely. If you think there are four great ideas out there, it's often too risky to launch all four of them at once. So a Bellissimo-size business typically generates one or two new products a year. Growth is important, but sensible growth is the key. We've never been satisfied to say, *Now we have 12 products, so let's coast for a while.* I've always understood the principle that you either continue to grow or you die. There's nothing in between. That principle works both in life and in business.

Vic: So your assumptions are that the conception of a project is mainly right-brain activity, and making sure there's a cash flow to support it is primarily left-brain activity. And in business it's that combination of right and left brain that's important to both growth and survival.

Bruce: Pretty much. There are certainly right-brain components involved in bringing a project to fruition. But small business is a juggling act. The creativity of making something happen is a juggling act.

For example: working with a local cameraman on a video and giving him a percentage of the video, rather than hiring him on a time-and-materials basis, ended up costing Bellissimo many thousands of dollars. Your left brain might say: *Hiring him would have been the smarter way to go.* But your right brain might ask: *Would that project have ever been done? Would it have ever been started, since it was the low financial risk at the front end that allowed us to take an idea and turn it into a reality?*

Vic: And would the finished product have had the quality you want?

Bruce: That's a good point, because the outcome is different when your name is involved. When you're not just a hired hand, you know that the quality of the product is going to reflect in the amount of sales and the benefit you're going to receive, as opposed to going to a job and putting your time in.

Business is complex. We can't just look back at that situation and say, *We should have hired this cameraman, and we'd have him paid off in a year rather than pay him over the probable ten-year life of the product.* That's the glass-is-half-empty scenario. The glass-is-half-full scenario is, *It worked; it was successful.*

The more creative you are in business—which involves a willingness to allow your imagination to flower and to accept taking risks that the left side of your brain wouldn't take—the better your advantage.

It's All Small Stuff

Vic: We've covered a lot of ground. By way of conclusion, is there a particular assumption that stands out for you, that shapes your life in the world of small business?

Bruce: One thing I've learned about the game of business is not to take yourself or it too seriously. I learned that years ago from the CEO of a company with hundreds of employees in a Midwestern town near which I had grown up. We had gone to competing high schools, so we had that in common. He owns his own airplane and three or four small airports around the country, and to say he's been successful as a small businessman would be the understatement of the year.

One day, as a friend, I sat down with him in his office, with the door closed. We talked for an hour or so, mainly about business philosophy. He described business as a battle, as a war, and the game was what drove him every day. And in the years since, he's acquired a number of his competitors, so he's continuing to be successful. But that day he said one thing to me I've never forgotten: *The main thing I have to realize and I try to make my employees realize is that if we went away tomorrow, nobody would ever miss us!*

We're not that important. This is not important.

Vic: It's all small stuff.

Bruce: It's all very small stuff. No matter how big it gets to be in life, no matter who you are, it's all quite insignificant in the big picture, the world view. And that's not to say you shouldn't take what you're doing seriously and give it 110 percent, but in the larger scheme of things, it's small stuff.

I'm reminded of the chapter where you wrote about what you want to do with the remaining years of your life, and I think that we who are creative spirits are in the best position. We have certain goals and aspirations that we would like to achieve while we're still here on earth. There are certain things we want to share with people, much of which entails communication. That's mostly what we're really talking about here. For those of us in the communicative field it's about our passion and about communicating that passion to the best of our ability. Whether it be via the Internet, giving talks at professional organizations, writing books, making films, producing music or taking photographs, it is the desire to share, educate and enlighten.

I suspect in most cases, people haven't found that passion yet. They're not living out their passion. I see the biggest task people face is finding their passion—seeking it out within themselves, identifying it and giving voice to it. I believe that most of us have a passion somewhere, a fire that can be lit and exploited for good.

Vic: Amen.

WHAT TO DO ABOUT THEM

Following is a listing of some of the assumptions that Bruce identifies as operating for him in the world of small business. How do they compare with some of yours?

- (I assume that) *business is a chess game. You have to train yourself to think in the manner of "the third move" and not the move you are making right now.*
- (I assume that) *in a particular situation, focusing on the two points of positive rather than the eight points of negative is the more productive option.*
- (I assume that) *when things really seem as if there's no way to solve a problem, often it can be solved. You just have to figure out how to get from point A to point C.*
- I really believe (assume) *people can do just about anything they want to do.*
- (I assume) *many people in business are always looking at the small picture.*
- (I assume) *to be successful, a small-business owner has to be extremely savvy, be able to think quickly, and see the big picture.*
- (I assume that) *success or failure in a small- or medium-sized business is determined mainly by attitude and thought processes.*
- (I assume that) *in business, the more creative you are—the more you are willing to allow your imagination to flower and to accept taking risks that the left side of your brain might not take—the better your advantage.*
- *I've always understood (assumed) that you either continue to grow or you die. There's nothing in between. That principle works both in life and in business.*

Notes & Comments

Notes & Comments

Notes & Comments

13

Assumptive Clusters

A Further Reach

Topic Index

13

Assumptive Clusters

A Further Reach

This final chapter introduces you to a deeper understanding of how our assumptions can shape our personalities and the various roles that we play in our daily lives.

I'm including it for two reasons: First, because it can inform you about a fascinating concept that suggests there's a good deal more to learn about assumptions and how they operate than we've covered in this book. Second, because it provides a meaningful bridge to a forthcoming book of mine, the working title of which is *Persona Work*.

This chapter will stretch your understanding of how assumptions work with a conceptual leap that looks at how groups of our compatible assumptions gather together in mutually supportive arrangements—which I call clusters—and how these assumptive clusters fashion different aspects of our personality. And while we'll be probing a bit more deeply into the realm of psychological theory, if you've kept pace with what's been said so far, you're ready to give this chapter a try.

Assumptive Clusters and How They Work

Think of an assumptive cluster as a baseball or soccer team.

The team consists of a group of individuals who work and play together. The team players support each other, depend upon each other, and feel strong bonds of loyalty and commitment. Players who don't follow the team rules and who aren't loyal to the team's goals don't make this particular team and have to find another team to play with.

An assumptive cluster operates in a similar fashion. All of the assumptions in a cluster work together and rely upon each other for support. And as on a team, assumptions that are at odds with the rules and beliefs of a particular team have to find some other team to play with.

If the concept of a team doesn't make sense for you, how about a political party?

If you're a loyal Republican, you subscribe to a particular set of Republican beliefs and positions that sets you apart from loyal Democrats. At the ballot box you vote for your party and its candidates, perhaps you participate in party activities, and, when asked, you identify yourself as *a Republican!*

Teams and political parties are powerful mechanisms without which we couldn't function in the world as we know it. And just as any team or political party is a way of organizing ourselves for collective action and effectiveness, an assumptive cluster is a way of organizing our assumptions.

Assumptive clusters are far more powerful and effective than any one assumption acting on its own. Our assumptive clusters are what drive us to succeed or to defend or to hold onto with our utmost commitment and zeal. They are why it can be extremely difficult to persuade others to think or behave differently from the way they do.

How Many Assumptive Clusters Do You Have?

Just as being a New York Yankee or being a Republican is only a small part of who we are as a person, any assumptive cluster of ours does not stand alone. It is but one of several or perhaps many.

The simplest way of thinking about assumptive clusters is to equate them with the social roles that we play. For example: If you're a Mom or a Dad, there is a cluster of particular attitudes, beliefs, values, emotional responses and behaviors that are closely associated with your Mom- or Dad-hood. You can easily draw up a list of them:

I will protect and defend my children with my life, if need be.
I will nurture them to the very best of my ability.
Nothing else is of greater importance to me than my children.

And so forth.

Taken as a whole, your list becomes a cluster of related and interdependent assumptions whose powerful impact and control over your life may be greater than anything else you can imagine.

Still, it does not by any stretch represent the whole of you. There are also the social roles of Wife or Husband (if you're married), Employee (if you have a job), Student (if you're taking classes), Actor (if you're in a theater group), Party-goer (if you're socially active), Little Girl or Little Boy (when you indulge your inner child), and so on and so forth. And each of your social roles is defined and shaped by the particular assumptions that attach to it. Your *Little Girl* or *Little Boy* will only come to life for you when you allow yourself to accept all the assumptions that go along with her or him, such as:

It's okay for me to manifest . . .
This is fun . . .
This is safe . . .
I can get away with this . . .

Whatever.

And, of course, there are other assumptions of yours that attach to your *Little Girl* or *Little Boy* that define them for you and shape how you feel about them. Your *Little Girl* may think she's pretty or ugly, smart or stupid, good or bad, fearless or fearful, or any number of other attributes and qualities. Much the same can be said of your *Little Boy.* We are all complex and, for the most part, easy descriptions—like clothes off the rack—may not exactly fit.

So we all have our assumptive clusters floating about in our heads. As we generate new assumptions, for the most part they rapidly become team players for the particular assumptive clusters that are most compatible to them. A Mom's fresh assumption about what's best for her children attaches itself to the cluster that defines and delineates the Mom social role. A new way of understanding one's role of Student, attaches to that cluster, and so on. As a rule, assumptions do not exist for long, if at all, by themselves but attach to the clusters that offer them the best support and reinforcement.

How many assumptive clusters do you have? Probably as many as the number of social roles that you play out in your life. And how many might that be? I wouldn't know, but it would make for an interesting assignment if you were to make a list of all the social roles you are aware of during the course of a day, or week, or month.

Assumptive Clusters and Personas

At the top of this chapter I referred to a meaningful connection between this book about assumptions and my forthcoming book, *Persona Work.*

What will that next book be about? Very simply: *How to work with our personas to build better and happier lives for ourselves.*

And what are our *personas?* They are the various aspects of our personality. They are the parts we play in the drama of our lives. They are the various facets and dimensions of who we are. They are the social role-players we select to articulate and express ourselves.

Aside from all the nonsense and folderol around *multiple personality syndromes, split-personalities,* and the like, we all have collections of different personas. They are essential basic equipment with which we manage to make our way through life. We generate and develop our personas to get for ourselves all that we believe we need. When we fail to recognize and use our personas well and wisely, we suffer in a variety of ways that *Persona Work* makes clear.

And what is the meaningful connection between my two books?

In my view of things, *Assumptive Clusters* are another way of understanding and describing *Personas*.

My many years of working with people and their personas have led me to believe that the two concepts are interchangeable. *Assumptive Clusters* and *Personas* are two ways of understanding and talking about the same phenomena. Your personas are your various players acting out their different social roles built around their own assumptive clusters. They may argue among themselves or fight over who gets to be in charge of your behavior but each contributes to who you are.

When you come right down to the nitty-gritty, it's all those assumptions and assumptive clusters and personas of yours that are responsible for making your particular choices and living out your own inimitable unique life.

So pay attention to them and learn and grow.

14

On To Your Future

In the Introduction I wrote: *I hope you find this book to be a powerful assist in your quest.* If indeed you are reading this after having worked your way through the rest of the book, the chances are very good that you have already fashioned useful tools to help you on your way.

If we were in a classroom or workshop together, this would the logical place to ask, *Do you have any questions?* and *Do you have thoughts you would like to share with the rest of us?* This is the part of a workshop I love most because your responses always stimulate me to explore fresh territory and learn new stuff I hadn't thought about before. I find Q&A sessions far more challenging than teaching material I know by heart.

And as fortune would have it, in this age of the Internet you are no more than a few clicks away from asking your questions and sharing your ideas—and I invite you to do exactly that.

You can reach me at my e-mail address: *vicbogart@aol.com* or web site: *Http://www.bogeybooks.com.*

Let me know what you think about the book, what you've learned, what the book's strong points and shortcomings are for you, and anything else that you wish to say to me. I welcome you all and look forward to hearing from you.

Thank you for being here with me and for allowing me to share with you. So on to your future! And my very best wishes to you on your quest.

Victor Bogart.